P9-DGR-202

The Andrew R. Cecil Lectures on

Moral Values in a Free Society

established by

The University of Texas at Dallas

Volume XVI

Previous Volumes of the Andrew R. Cecil Lectures on Moral Values in a Free Society

Volume I: The Third Way (1979)
Volume II: The Ethics of Citizenship (1980)
Volume III: Conflict and Harmony (1981)
Volume IV: The Search for Justice (1982)
Volume V: The Citizen and His Government (1983)
Volume VI: Our Freedoms: Rights and Responsibilities (1984)
Volume VII: A Melting Pot or a Nation of Minorities (1985)
Volume VIII: Traditional Moral Values in the Age of Technology (1986)
Volume IX: Democracy: Its Strengths and Weaknesses (1987)
Volume X: Religion and Politics (1988)
Volume XI: Our Economic System: Its Strengths and Weaknesses (1989)
Volume XII: The Meaning of the Family in a Free Society (1990)
Volume XIII: Morality and Expediency in International and Corporate Relations (1991)
Volume XIV: The Morality of the Mass Media (1992)
Volume XV: Individualism and Social Responsibility (1993)

The Foundations of a Free Society by Andrew R. Cecil
Three Sources of National Strength by Andrew R. Cecil
Equality, Tolerance, and Loyalty by Andrew R. Cecil

MORAL VALUES IN LIBERALISM AND CONSERVATISM

Moral Values in Liberalism and Conservatism

ANDREW R. CECIL
JAMES TOBIN
DICK ARMEY
EDWARD J. HARPHAM
WILSON CAREY McWILLIAMS

With an Introduction by
ANDREW R. CECIL

Edited by
W. LAWSON TAITTE

The University of Texas at Dallas
1995

Printed in the United States of America

Library of Congress Catalog Card Number 95-060717
International Standard Book Number 0-292-78139-3

Distributed by the University of Texas Press,
Box 7819, Austin, Texas 78712

CONTENTS

FOREWORD

In 1979, the University of Texas at Dallas established the Andrew R. Cecil Lectures on Moral Values in a Free Society to provide a forum for the discussion of important issues that face our society. Each year since, U.T. Dallas has invited to its campus scholars, businessmen and members of the professions, public officials, and other notable individuals to share their ideas on this subject with the academic community and the general public. During the sixteen years of their existence, the Cecil Lectures have become a valued tradition for the University and for the wider community. The presentations of the many distinguished authorities who have participated in the program have enriched the experience of all those who heard them or read the published proceedings of each series. They have enlarged our understanding of the system of moral values on which our country was founded and continues to rest.

The University named this program for Dr. Andrew R. Cecil, its Distinguished Scholar in Residence. During his tenure as President of The Southwestern Legal Foundation, Dr. Cecil's innovative leadership brought that institution into the forefront of continuing legal education in the United States.

When he retired from the Foundation as its Chancellor Emeritus, Dr. Cecil was asked by U.T. Dallas to serve as its Distinguished Scholar in Residence, and the Cecil Lectures were instituted. In 1990, the Board of Regents of The University of Texas System established the Andrew R. Cecil Chair of Applied Ethics. It is appropriate that the Lectures and the Chair honor a man who has been concerned throughout his career with the moral foundations of our society and has stressed his belief in the dignity and worth of every individual.

The sixteenth annual series of the Cecil Lectures was held on the University's campus on November 7 through 10, 1994. It examined the theme of "Moral Values in Liberalism and Conservatism." On behalf of U.T. Dallas, I would like to express our appreciation to Congressman Dick Armey, Professor James Tobin, Professor Wilson Carey McWilliams, Professor Edward J. Harpham, and Dr. Cecil for their willingness to share their ideas and for the outstanding lectures that are preserved in this volume of proceedings.

I also wish to express on behalf of the University our sincere gratitude to all those who have helped make this program an important part of the life of the University, especially the contributors to the Lectures. Through their support these donors enable us to continue this important program and to publish the proceedings of the series, thus assuring a wide and permanent audience for the ideas the books contain.

I am confident that everyone who reads *Moral Values in Liberalism and Conservatism*, the Andrew R. Cecil Lectures on Moral Values in a Free Society Volume XVI, will be stimulated by the ideas expressed there so eloquently.

FRANKLYN G. JENIFER, President
The University of Texas at Dallas
March 1995

INTRODUCTION

by

Andrew R. Cecil

"The ultimate aim of government is not to rule, or restrain, by fear, nor to exact obedience, but contrariwise, to free every man from fear, that he may live in all possible security; in other words, to strengthen his natural right to exist and work without injury to himself or others.

"No, the object of government is not to change men from rational beings into beasts or puppets, but to enable them to develop their minds and bodies in security, and to employ their reason unshackled; neither showing hatred, anger, or deceit, nor watched with the eyes of jealousy and injustice. In fact, the true aim of government is liberty." (Benedictus de Spinoza, "Tractatus Theologico-Politicus," *Writings on Political Philosophy*, ed. by A.G.A. Balz, trans. R.H.M. Elwes, D. Appleton-Century Company, 1937, p. 65.)

What does it mean to be a liberal or a conservative? In tracing the etymological development of these terms we find that in Latin *liberare* means to set free; similarly, in French *libre* means free.

Conservare in Latin means to preserve; in French the *conservateur* was an official responsible for protection of certain rights and charged with the guardianship of certain public property.

At present, "conservative" and "liberal" are used as contrasting terms. All too often we hear them used in a pejorative sense: Liberals are identified with "leftist" radicals, and conservatives are blamed for their "reactionary" positions aimed at preserving the traditional and rejecting innovations.

The contemporary usage of the terms "liberal" and "conservative" differs dramatically from the connotations attached to them in the eighteenth and nineteenth centuries. As the idea of liberalism emerged, it was deeply affected by the growth of individualism, which had developed and expanded under the impact of cultural and intellectual currents of the Renaissance and the Reformation. John Locke and John Stuart Mill, among others, provided its philosophical foundations.

The name "Conservative" was attached to a political party in England for the first time in 1830. The conservatives under this banner were dedicated to preserving—within the framework of traditional values—monarchical and aristocratic privileges. They entrusted leadership to the established and experienced social group or class, thus rejecting the concept of universal equality of opportunity for each individual regardless of his social origin.

The founders of political liberalism, on the other hand, argued for the freedom of each individual to develop himself as a human being. Such freedom comprises liberty of thought and opinion and association—most notably the liberty to speak, write. and unite. In classical liberalism, the use of power by the government was justified only in order to prevent harm to others.

The political ideas of conservatism in their early stages did not differ from the doctrine of liberalism advocated, for instance, by John Stuart Mill in his essay *On Liberty*. The role of government as described by Abraham Lincoln appealed to the early advocates of liberalism. Today, however, it seems closer to the views of contemporary conservatives. President Lincoln wrote:

> "The legitimate object of government is to do for a community of people whatever they need to have done but cannot do *at all*, or cannot *so well* do, for themselves—in their separate and individual capacities. In all that the people can individually do as well for themselves, government ought not to interfere." (*The Collected Works of Abraham Lincoln*, ed. Roy P. Basler, Rutgers University Press, 1953, pp. 220-221.)

One hundred years later, President Lyndon B. Johnson ascribed to the government a much broader role. "I believe that the essence of government," he stated, "lies with unceasing concern for the welfare and dignity and decency and innate integrity of life for every individual . . . regardless of color, creed, ancestry, sex, or age." (Remarks at a civil rights symposium, LBJ Library, Austin, Texas, December 12, 1972, p. 1.)

Whether it is claimed by modern liberals or conservatives, the original concept of liberalism has been distorted. Liberals these days have abandoned the idea, so much a part of the former tradition of liberalism, that the best government is the least government. Because of economic and political changes that have occurred in the last three centuries, the American conservative also cannot claim adherence to traditional liberalism. He has accepted the government's responsibility for numerous social programs, and the essence of his conservatism is to prevent the strengthening of the role of the government and the transformation of its limited powers into a paternalistic state.

The conflict between liberalism and conservatism transcends the boundaries of political life—to mention only the charges exchanged between the followers of liberal theology and fundamentalists. The fundamentalists profess to believe in the Bible verbatim from cover to cover. The liberals accept the Bible as a priceless heritage, a blueprint for life, but claim that some of its concepts belong to the distant past and cannot be bridged with the world today.

It is often hard to draw a line of demarcation between the liberals and the fundamentalists. St. Paul in all his evangelical zeal was also liberal in rejecting racial barriers for those who have faith. "I am not ashamed of the Gospel of Christ: for it is the power of God unto salvation of every one that believeth; for the Jew first and also the Greek." (Romans 1:16.) Martin Luther was liberal in his doctrine of "the priesthood of all believers." Although he protested against the mighty ecclesiastical imperialism of his day, as a German royalist he was also a fundamentalist in his support of the ruling classes in the Peasants' Revolt. We may add that Luther's conviction that a society should have unequal classes, that "some are free, others captives, some masters, others subjects," and his distrust of merchants and peasants relate to the economic conditions of the sixteenth century.

The fundamentalists and the liberals agree that the story of Jesus is a foundation of a new gospel of hope and life. The real conflict between them arises when the fundamentalists insist that they have a calling to reveal the truth divinely bestowed upon them while the liberals try to reduce Christianity to a mundane code of ethics.

Another area affected by the political ideologies of liberalism and conservatism that I bring up in my lecture, "Liberalism and Conservatism in Their Historical Development," is the administration of justice. One of the healthy manifestations of our ideals of justice is the nonpartisan administration of justice within our system. Politicians and commentators, however, apply the labels "liberal" and "conservative" to members of and candidates for the judiciary, depending upon a judge's attitude toward labor matters, civil rights, or governmental regulations.

As I stress in my lecture, the administration of justice should never be subordinated to political pressures. It should be based on disinterestedness and should be detached and safeguarded from political considerations. As Edmund Burke defined the concepts of law and justice: "There is but one law for all, namely that law which governs all law, the law of our Creator, the law of humanity, justice, equity—the Law of Nature and of Nations." (*Impeachment of Warren Hastings*, May 28, 1794.)

The meanings of the terms "liberal" and "conservative" have varied over the years. The reason that modern liberals and conservatives are no longer identified with the beliefs of liberalism and conservatism as originally conceived may be found in the dramatic economic, political, social, intellectual, and ideological challenges that have occurred since the eighteenth and nineteenth centuries. Professor James Tobin in his lecture, "Democratic Values and Capitalist Efficiency: The Liberal Reconciliation," and Congressman Dick Armey in his lecture, "The Invisible Foot of Government," discuss the moral values of contemporary liberalism and conservatism respectively.

Both examine the economic issues from a moral perspective. Professor Tobin acknowledges that capitalism, in the course of building an economy, naturally produces inequalities. He believes, however, that—within certain limits—greater economic equality is worth promoting in a democratic state. His lecture poses the question whether citizens of such a democracy should not be willing to sacrifice some of the efficiencies of capitalism in order to achieve greater equality and a higher standard of living for its poorer members.

Professor Tobin's own answer to his question is that such a trade-off is not only appropriate but desirable. But such a conclusion introduces another quandary: How much inefficiency should an economy tolerate to bring about greater equality? Although he acknowledges that each observer will answer this question differently, Professor Tobin seeks a golden mean. He cannot agree with the theorists who would advocate almost any sacrifice to achieve equality, but he argues for generosity in meeting the needs of the less fortunate.

Congressman Armey, on the other hand, argues that any interference with the workings of the marketplace produces hidden and highly undesirable consequences. Markets, he believes, are one of the great sources of progress in civilization—not only economic markets, which call for unfettered liberty of buyer and seller to bargain, but the political and spiritual arenas where ideas and values compete for the hearts and minds of citizens. Limiting such liberty in any way introduces distortions that ultimately work to the detriment of all involved.

The classical statement of this principle is embodied in Adam Smith's doctrine of the invisible hand of the market—the idea that each individual, acting out of selfish considerations, unwittingly works for the common good in each transaction in a free market situation. In Congressman Armey's scheme, the invisible hand of the market is coupled with a visible foot—the painful corrections the market makes when a given transaction or idea is unproductive. Both these aspects of the market are mirrored in reverse by actions of the government. The benefits of governmental intervention are quite visible—handouts and incentives awarded to a favored few. (Congressman Armey calls this the "visible hand of the government.") But the negative side effects of governmental action are hard to detect, though in his view they are disastrous. (These he terms "the visible foot of the government.")

As both Professor Tobin and Congressman Armey agree, society is a product of man's social nature. His needs are the ultimate foundation of all government; his interest in creating a system of government authority is to keep it in the service of society. The resulting governmental responsibility and services make social man a political man. As we have seen, the extent of governmental authority has become one of the most important areas of public policy—and a continuing source of intense debate.

The proper use of government may be essential to provide the environment in which society can flourish. The functions of government are no longer limited to national defense, fiscal and foreign policy, and restraint of antisocial individuals and groups. Everyone in our modern society seems to agree that it is the government's responsibility to preserve the lives of the members of our communities and protect them not only from physical violence but also from natural agents that threaten their health and well-being, such as floods, epidemics, and crippling diseases. Unemployment, the proliferation of slums, and the deterioration of our cities and of the natural environment also call for some form of governmental intervention.

On the other hand, there is indeed a danger of excessive government control. Today we have enough experience of what happens under totalitarian regimes built on the unlimited dominance of the executive authority to recognize the inherent dangers of unchecked power. In these situations, uncritical recourse to the state created economic and political serfdom. Having thus learned the disaster that excessive reliance on central authority can wreak, we are faced with the task of discerning just how much responsibility for the common good we can safely entrust to government. What is the proper role of the government in discharging its responsibilities for the welfare of the society and of the individual without depriving the people of their right to shape their destiny?

Even in the democracies of Europe, and to a lesser extent in Canada and the United States, the welfare system is under an enormous strain. Increases in life expectancy continue to push spending on social welfare upward—an aging population has a large impact on publicly provided pensions and health care. In addition, rising unemployment and an increasing number of low-income families (especially of the growing number of single-parent families) have added significantly to the cost of the welfare system. In the United States from 1988 through 1992, welfare spending by federal, state, and local government increased from $217 billion to $305 billion. The "welfare state," providing support "from the cradle to the grave," has fallen into disrepute, and the political pressure for fundamental reforms of the welfare system is gaining strength and popularity.

In his lecture "From Public Welfare to Private Virtue: Shifting Liberal and Conservative Concepts of Social Well-Being," Professor Edward J. Harpham traces the changes in ideas concerning the proper role of government in assisting citizens in their pursuit of happiness. Liberals, he argues, tend to define well-being largely in material terms. Conservatives, on the other hand, view attempts to assure economic equality as destroying the moral fiber of the nation.

Professor Harpham examines the effects the New Deal of the 1930s had on American ideas of social justice. Over the last fifty years, the powers of the government have expanded enormously. For much of that time, the premises on which this expansion was built were barely challenged in many circles. Simultaneously, however, a different philosophical outlook was being developed that stressed the importance of private virtue, rather than governmental mandate, in forming the good society.

History has demonstrated that doctrinaire solutions, including those claiming to resolve important political and economic issues, are limited to a certain place and time. They rise to eminence only to share a common fate—to be replaced or modified by new ideas. This is also true, as our lecturers have shown, of various theories of liberalism and conservatism.

As I pointed out in my lecture, from the early days of liberalism and conservatism there was always a profound difference between the American and the British understanding of these philosophies. In the United States, one of the prevailing values was respect for "self-made" men and for every individual's right to equality of opportunity. In Great Britain, class distinction, social origin, religious affiliation, and education were far more influential in molding political views and actions.

Although the Founding Fathers profoundly distrusted the party system, the United States evolved a working system of party government. Liberalism and conservatism, however, have never served as party creeds. We have liberal and conservative Democrats as well as liberal, moderate, and conservative Republicans. Since the lines of distinction between the platforms of the two parties are not clearly drawn, crosscurrents of liberalism and conservatism have flowed back and forth during the history of American political thought.

Professor Wilson Carey McWilliams in his lecture "Ambiguities and Ironies: Conservatism and Liberalism in the American Political Tradition" demonstrates how blurred the distinctions between liberalism and conservatism have always been in American political practice. Not only do both parties embrace aspects of what are generally considered the liberal and conservative creeds, almost every leader in those parties has taken stands that fall on both sides on the line dividing the two camps.

The ambiguities that Professor McWilliams points out include the American attitude toward capitalism. Although conservatives have been the great promulgators of a faith that capitalism is the road to prosperity and progress, Professor McWilliams finds it ironic that the nature of capitalism is not to preserve but to tear down old ways of life while building new ones. And conservatives have sought remedy for existing evils in governmental programs as readily as liberals, despite conservative distrust of big government.

In conclusion, let me say that the readers of this volume of proceedings will find that all the 1994 participants in the Lectures on Moral Values in a Free Society recognize the importance of political dialogue between those who hold opposite views. Only through constructive dialogue can we build the bridge between self-interest—the moving spirit of free enterprise and conservatism—and the general interest, which may call for the governmental action advocated by liberalism and for the moderation of self-interest. Unless our political life is undergirded by a desire to build such a bridge, our society will be pulled back and forth between political contradictions that continue to divide us.

LIBERALISM AND CONSERVATISM IN THEIR HISTORICAL DEVELOPMENT

by

Andrew R. Cecil

Andrew R. Cecil

Andrew R. Cecil is Distinguished Scholar in Residence at The University of Texas at Dallas. The University established in his honor the Andrew R. Cecil Lectures on Moral Values in a Free Society in February 1979 and invited Dr. Cecil to deliver the first series of lectures in November of that year. The first annual proceedings were published as Dr. Cecil's book The Third Way: Enlightened Capitalism and the Search for a New Social Order, *which received an enthusiastic response. He has also lectured in each subsequent series. A new book,* The Foundations of a Free Society, *was published in 1983.* Three Sources of National Strength *appeared in 1986, and* Equality, Tolerance, and Loyalty *in 1990. In 1976 the University named for Dr. Cecil the Andrew R. Cecil Auditorium, and in 1990 it established the Andrew R. Cecil Endowed Chair in Applied Ethics.*

Educated in Europe and well launched on a career as a professor and practitioner in the fields of law and economics, Dr. Cecil resumed his academic career after World War II in Lima, Peru, at the University of San Marcos. After 1949, he was associated with the Methodist church-affiliated colleges and universities in the United States until he joined The Southwestern Legal Foundation in 1958. Dr. Cecil helped guide the development of the Foundation's five educational centers that offer nationally and internationally recognized programs in advanced continuing education. Since his retirement as President of the Foundation, he serves as Chancellor Emeritus and Honorary Trustee.

Dr. Cecil is author of fifteen books on the subjects of law, economics, and religion and of more than seventy articles on these subjects and on the philosophy of religion published in periodicals and anthologies. A member of the American Society of International Law, of the American Branch of the International Law Association, and of the American Judicature Society, Dr. Cecil has served on numerous commissions for the Methodist Church and is a member of the Board of Trustees of the National Methodist Foundation for Christian Higher Education. In 1981 he was named an Honorary Rotarian.

LIBERALISM AND CONSERVATISM IN THEIR HISTORICAL DEVELOPMENT

by

Andrew R. Cecil

The Fallibility of Doctrines

Each age produces men with visions of a more perfect society, who frequently offer dramatically opposed paths that they hope will lead to prosperity and political stability. At one extreme, we have apologists for strong limitation of the functions of government and for free competition in economic affairs; at the other, apologists for an all-powerful totalitarian social and economic order.

We have also witnessed that, throughout history, doctrinaire solutions that attempted to dominate real life with abstract principles have proven erroneous and impracticable when confronted with the reality of modern life, where many new factors have been present and old ones absent. This common fate of doctrinaire solutions leads to the conclusion that political and economic theories are limited to a certain place and time; they rise to eminence only to fall and be replaced or drastically modified by other theories, which, themselves, eventually will follow the same pattern. This is also true about the theories known as liberalism and conservatism.

Before discussing the moral values and merits of liberalism and conservatism in their historical development, let me illustrate the ascent and eventual fall of some of the theories on governmental functions that originated in Europe in the seventeenth and eighteenth centuries.

In the seventeenth century in Great Britain, the economic principles of mercantilism superseded the medieval feudal organization of society. Following the assumption that there is a basic conflict between the national interest and the interests of the individual, mercantilism called for a powerful government and for its strong intervention in a nation's economic life. A nation, according to the mercantilists, is enriched by an influx of precious metals and impoverished by their export. Such an influx can only be achieved by a favorable balance of trade that takes place when a nation sells other nations more than it buys abroad. To obtain such a trade balance, the government sought complete control over production, trade, commodity prices, rents, interest rates, and profits. (The restrictive measures that the British parliament placed on the economic life of the American colonies were part of its mercantile policies.)

The economic principles of mercantilism were modified in the eighteenth century by the physiocrats and later strongly opposed by the advocates of *laissez-faire*. The most direct precursor of Adam

Smith's idea of natural liberty, whereby each individual by following his own interest promotes social welfare, was the doctrine of the physiocrats or *economistes* of France. Headed by Francois Quesnay (1694–1774), they advocated the least possible governmental interference with industry and business. They believed, however, that only absolute monarchy can safeguard a society from its internal conflicts. They also advocated the single tax on land, since in their opinion only agriculture provided economic surpluses, and income from all other occupations, including manufacturing (which they considered "sterile"), derived from the income of land. (In the United States, Henry George in his *Progress and Poverty* also argued as late as 1879 that all taxes should be levied on land.)

In reaction to the mercantilist and physiocrat doctrines, the *laissez-faire-laissez-aller* philosophy emphasized the importance of freedom of competition with strong limitations on the functions of government. In the absence of restrictions, it was argued, all factors of production would be employed to produce maximum gains, with consequent profit both to society and to the individual. According to the law of comparative advantage, a nation tends to export those goods which it can produce at relatively low costs and to import those goods for which its costs of production are relatively high. Consequently, all restrictions on trade between nations should be eliminated.

Adam Smith (1723–1790) promulgated these ideas in his famous *The Wealth of Nations*, the first systematic exposition of economics, which is the bible of capitalism and the beginning of modern economics. In it, he proclaimed freedom of enterprise as the "obvious and simple system of natural liberty." Taking the concept of natural liberty far beyond free trade in Book Five of *The Wealth of Nations*, he applied it also to education and religion. If only free competition could operate, Smith maintained, an "invisible hand" would lead to a harmonious order that would work to the benefit of all. The invisible hand, according to Smith, promotes economic development, and its "price-profit equilibrium mechanism" prompts the production of goods that people want at prices they are ready to pay.

History has given ample evidence that when the philosophy of private enterprise becomes dogmatic and absolute, the "natural order" of a completely uncontrolled process of a free economy causes massive human suffering. The Industrial Revolution was characterized in its beginning by a brutal contempt for human life, reckless exploitation of men, women, and children, and shocking inhumanities. Rampant individualism, unheedingly striving for personal gain, resulted in great social injustices.

In reaction to this appalling record of inhumanity, the socialists found their prophet in Karl Marx (1818–1883) and their bible in his chief work: *Das Kapital*. Ignoring the role of the entrepreneur, Karl Marx and Friedrich Engels in their *Manifesto of the*

Communist Party (1848) called upon their followers to hasten by revolution the "inevitable event of the collapse of capitalism." They concluded their manifesto with an appeal: "Let the ruling class tremble at a communist revolution. The proletarians have nothing to lose but their chains. They have a world to win."

What kind of a world did the communists offer the "proletarians"? Slavery was revived in the form of concentration camps, with millions of prisoners jailed to furnish unpaid labor so that the state had no need to provide the minimum of goods that free workers expect. The omnipotent state that suppressed all opposition produced diabolical outrages against human personality.

Outside the communist states, the capitalist system survived, but even in the countries that profess to live under the capitalist system, the economic scene has drastically changed from the order conceived by Adam Smith. Doctrines that strive to possess the soul of man's economic, political, and even spiritual life are found upon examination to be limited in their application to the period and place when and where they rose to eminence. They share a common fate: They are replaced or modified by new ideas. This is also true of the theories of liberalism and conservatism.

In the modern age that began with the Renaissance and the Reformation, a new science emerged and became known as political economy. In it, economic life and the scope of public action were acknowledged to be interwoven with each other and inseparable. (Book IV of *The Wealth of Nations* deals with the "System of Political Economy.") With the rise of the modern state, economic affairs came to be seen as interrelated with the individual's political rights protecting him from abuses by those in authority over him.

This interrelationship was stressed by the emerging proponents of liberalism. To illustrate this connection, we might point out that Thomas Jefferson's Declaration of Independence proclaiming political freedom was written at nearly the same time that Adam Smith first expressed the revolutionary idea of economic freedom.

The Growth of Individualism

Individualism, which during the fourteenth to sixteenth centuries grew out of the cultural and intellectual currents of the Renaissance and the Reformation, paved the way for the birth of liberalism in the eighteenth century. Out of the Reformation came Protestantism, which put emphasis upon the dignity of the individual. It proclaimed that, by reason of the doctrine of the priesthood of all believers, individuals had inherent rights and privileges. Protestantism revolted against ecclesiastical imperialism by affirming that God is accessible to individual approaches.

According to Martin Luther, in matters concerning salvation of souls, "each one must for himself stand before God and give account." He proclaimed that God speaks as a voice in the heart of each individual and not through the mediation of the priesthood. The principle that the individual layman could understand "God's Word," the scripture, with no need of a priest to interpret it for him, lent dignity and worth to those who dissented from certain views and practices of the existing ecclesiastical authority of the time.

In its rebellion against the medieval ecclesiastical control of political and economic as well as spiritual life, Protestantism came to make a great contribution to the assertion of the importance of individual rights. It laid the foundation for the eventual separation of church and state and performed an incomparable task in the history of Western civilization by proclaiming the right of the individual to the free exercise of religion and the right to equal opportunities in political, economic, and social life.

The Rise of Liberalism

Animated by the desire for such individual rights, the second half of the seventeenth century and the eighteenth century—known as the Age of Enlightenment and also as the Age of Reason—were marked by the hostile reaction of the British and French philosophers and writers against political and ecclesiastical absolutism, the customs and institutions of the established authorities. From the interaction of ideas among these philosophers and writers, to mention only John Locke (1632–1704) in England and Denis Diderot (1713–1784) and Francois Voltaire (1694–1778) in France, emerged confidence in the power of reason to prepare the way for social, political, and moral progress. The thinkers of the eighteenth century paved the way to progress with liberal concepts of man's right to personal freedom, to dissent, and to pursue his own interest with the greatest amount of individual liberty from governmental interference. Liberalism was the child of the Age of Reason—the Enlightenment.

The influence of Locke was exceedingly great. It spread widely in eighteenth-century Europe and had an impact not only on the British system of government but also on the ideals of the American Revolution of 1776. It has been asserted that the liberalism of the eighteenth and nineteenth centuries stemmed largely from this important English philosopher. His ideas on natural law contributed to the newborn ideas of freedom of thought and of a government limited in its power and based firmly on the consent of the governed. Locke's conception of a fiduciary relationship between free individuals and their rulers, with the government having the duties of a trustee and the community enjoying the rights of a beneficiary, appealed to the liberals of the eighteenth century. They stressed the independence, freedoms, and equality with which individuals are endowed by nature.

In the eighteenth century, the great mind of Adam Smith laid the foundation for the idea of individual natural liberty from governmental authority. In the closing decades of the eighteenth century and in the nineteenth century two major names mark the rise of liberalism in England: Jeremy Bentham (1748–1832) and John Stuart Mill (1806-1873).

Bentham contributed to the theory that the goal of society and the criterion of morality is the greatest good (summum bonum) and happiness for the greatest number. This theory, known as utilitarianism, with its claims that the individual's happiness depends upon the happiness of "the greatest number," preceded the development of modern democracy. Bentham's approach to morals and legislation, which made him famous throughout the world, was expressed in his desire to humanize the law: "The general object which all laws have, or ought to have, in common, is to augment the total happiness of the community." (*Principles of Morals and Legislation*, 1789.) Bentham's utilitarianism can be described as the ethics of enlightened self-interest seeking happiness as an end in itself. Self-interest or self-realization involves an individual's pursuit of his ideals and ambitions, a pursuit satisfying to him and at the same time useful to the society in which he lives.

John Stuart Mill

Utilitarianism is associated above all with the name of the English philosopher and economist, John Stuart Mill. Among political writers, Mill was the most widely known for his attempts to determine the proper rights and limits for individual action and for governmental interference in private affairs.

He received a rigorous education from his father James Mill, an ardent Benthamite. James Mill was an exacting teacher. John was taught Greek at the age of three, and he had read Plato at the age of eight, when he also began to study Latin. When he was about thirteen years old, he took a course in political economy, during which he read Adam Smith and Ricardo. At the age of fourteen, he spent a year in France with the family of Jeremy Bentham's brother, General Sir Samuel Bentham, studying the French language and French literature.

Upon his return to London, John Stuart Mill's education and experience included discussions with members of the Benthamite circle that shaped his mind to become the moving spirit of the group known as the utilitarians. They were dedicated to promoting the principle of "Utility" or the "Greatest Happiness Principle."

According to this principle, actions are right when they promote happiness, wrong as they tend to produce pain. Happiness is equated with pleasure; unhappiness, pain or privation from pleasure. Mill regarded utility as "the ultimate appeal on all ethical questions; but it must be utility in the largest sense, grounded on the permanent interests of man as a progressive being." (*On Liberty*, ed. by Currin V. Shields, Library of Liberal Arts, 1956, p. 14.) According to Mill, these interests are subject to external control only with respect to those actions which affect the interests of other people.

Mill's utilitarianism is not a philosophy of expediency or egoism that serves the interest of the individual without regard to the common good. His concept of freedom does not mean merely freedom from coercion and governmental control. His teaching differs from that of the Benthamites in stressing that happiness cannot be pursued as an end in itself but should be the result of purposeful conduct. The individual's conduct is purposeful when it leads to the development of his personality and of all his powers that may contribute to the common good. Disillusioned with the beliefs advocated by Bentham, Mill in his *Utilitarianism* abandoned the dogmas of Benthamism by drawing his famous distinction between quantity and quality of pleasure, since some kinds of pleasure are more desirable and more valuable than others.

So much for the utility theory. The purpose of my lecture is not to discuss the intricacies of this theory. I only mentioned it to give a background for Mill's most famous political writing—his essay *On Liberty*, which epitomizes the nineteenth-century British ideas on liberalism.

Mill's primary concern is to find the nature and limits of the power which can be legitimately exercised by society over the individual. This concern is justified by the fact that "the struggle between liberty and authority is the most conspicuous feature in the portion of history" which goes back to early times in Greece and Rome. Because of this struggle, liberty "means protection against the tyranny of the political rulers." (*Id.*, p. 3.) In his attempt to define the limits within which a person can pursue his interest, Mill reached the following conclusions: a) Individual freedom is justified by a contribution to the general interest; concurrent with the individual's right to freedom is his duty to take a fair share in discharging society's responsibilities; b) the use of the power of government over individuals is justified only in order to prevent harm to others; society has jurisdiction over individuals' actions that affect the interests of others.

The individual's own good, either physical or moral, is not "a sufficient warrant" for the exercise of coercion by the community. The only freedom which deserves that name is, according to Mill, "that of pursuing our own good in our own way, so long as we do not attempt to deprive others of theirs or impede their efforts to obtain it." (*Id.*, pp. 16–17.) Mill's liberty means freedom to develop oneself as a human being. Such freedom contributes to the common good, and society, therefore, has no right to put up obstacles to such development.

What constitutes human liberty? First, liberty of conscience in the most comprehensive sense: liberty of thought and freedom of opinion and sentiment "on all subjects, practical or speculative, scientific, moral, or theological." Related to liberty of thought is liberty of speaking and writing. No government has the right to control the expression of opinion even if this control is exerted in accordance with public opinion. "If all mankind minus one were of one opinion, mankind would be no more justified in silencing the one person than he, if he had power, would be justified in silencing mankind." (*Id.*, p. 21.)

Second, liberty of tastes and pursuits, so long as our actions do not harm our fellowmen, "even though they should think that our conduct is foolish, perverse, or wrong." Third, "freedom to unite for any purpose not involving harm to others." (*Id.*, p. 16.) Whenever rulers infringed on the individual's political liberties or rights, "specific resistance or general rebellion was held to be justifiable." (*Id.*, p. 4.)

The weaker members of the community, Mill maintained, are being preyed upon by innumerable vultures, but the ruler, "the king of the vultures," stronger than the rest and commissioned to keep them down, is "no less bent upon preying on the flock than any of the minor harpies." It is indispensable, therefore, to be "in perpetual attitude of defense against his beak and claws." (*Id.*, p. 4.) In order to limit the power of the rulers, whose interests are frequently opposed to those of the people, Mill suggested establishing constitutional checks to control the acts of the governing power and periodically electing various magistrates, their terms revocable at the pleasure of the governed. In this way the interest of the rulers will be identified with the interest and will of the people.

Can democracy provide conditions for harmony between the interest of the people and the interest of the rulers? Mill, undoubtedly influenced by Alexis de Tocqueville, the celebrated author of *Democracy in America*, shared his fear of the dangers of the binding power of the majority under popular rule. Tocqueville warned:

> "If ever freedom is lost in America, that will be due to the omnipotence of the majority driving the minorities to desperation and forcing them to appeal to physical force. We may then see anarchy, but it will come as the result of despotism." (*Democracy in America*, ed. by J. P. Mayer and Max Lerner, Harper & Row, 1966, p. 240.)

It seems that Tocqueville himself dispelled his fear that the rule of the majority could turn into legal tyranny when he defined the dogma of the sovereignty of the people in the United States:

> "In the United States the dogma of the sovereignty of the people is not an isolated doctrine, bearing no relation to the people's habits and prevailing ideas; . . . Providence has given each individual the amount of reason necessary for him to look after himself in matters of his own exclusive concern. That is the great maxim on which civil and political society in the United States rests; the father of a family applies it to his children, a master to his servants, a township to

> those under its administration, a province to the townships, a state to the provinces, and the Union to the states. Extended to the nation as a whole, it becomes the dogma of the sovereignty of the people." (*Id.*, p. 364.)

Mill remained hostile to the tyranny of the majority of the common people—"the uncultivated herd who now comprise the laboring masses"—over the minority of individuals who meet Mill's standard of intellectual development. Mill's liberalism can be described as a middle-class world view reflecting classical nineteenth-century British political ideas and the rise to power of a new social stratum. The middle-class reformers with their liberalism resented the political and social status of the landed aristocracy and shifted society's elite of land and birth to the elite of wealth and talent.

Mill's doctrine of liberalism shares the fate of other fallible dogmas described above. As we mentioned, doctrinaire solutions are limited to a certain place and time. Mill, referring to a rule of conduct, admitted that "No two ages, and scarcely any two countries, have decided it alike; and the decision of one age or country, is wonder to another." Furthermore, although he consistently stressed the maxim that the individual is not accountable to society for his actions insofar as these concern the interest of no persons but himself, on occasion he gave society astonishingly broad powers to interfere. Thus he accepted as an almost self-evident axiom that the state should require and compel the education, up to a certain standard, of every human being who is born its citizen. He declared that the state should extend aid to those unable to defray the expense of education and believed that public examination should serve as an instrument enforcing the law concerning compulsory education aimed at "retention of a certain minimum of general knowledge." (*On Liberty*, p. 130.)

There are other examples of what Mill believed to be legitimate interference of the state in the lives of individuals. If, in consequence of an oversupply of labor and reduced wages, it became apparent that parents are unable to support their children, he thought that a law to forbid marriages would not constitute a violation of liberty. He regarded legislation to reduce the hours of labor universally enforced by law to be legitimate. Although the principle of individual liberty is not involved in the doctrine of free trade, public control is admissible to prevent fraud, to protect workers employed in dangerous occupations, or to provide sanitary precautions. Persons are free to gamble in their own or each other's houses, but public gambling houses should not be permitted. Taxation of alcoholic beverages ("stimulants"), which produce the largest amount of revenue, "is not only admissible, but to be approved of." The laws forbidding marriages unless the parties can show that they have the means of supporting a family "do not exceed the legitimate powers of the State" and "are not objectionable as violation of liberty."

In absence of any recognized general principles of liberty, Mill saw no lack of consistency between his claims that "over himself, over his own body and mind, the individual is sovereign" and "that the state, while it respects the liberty of each individual, is bound to maintain a vigilant control over the individual's exercise of any power which it allows him to possess over others." (*Id.*, pp. 13 and 127.) By calling for such controls, Mill acknowledged that interference by the state may be necessary to protect the individual's rights to liberty.

It may be mentioned that Herbert Spencer (1820-1903), a contemporary of Mill considered by some the most prominent English philosopher of the nineteenth century, was much more extreme than Mill in his philosophical radicalism aimed at restricting the powers of the state and defending individual liberty. In his philosophy based on the principle of evolution, which he applied to every field of study including psychology, sociology, and ethics, Spencer concluded that the only function of the state is the administration of justice to prevent violation of the individual's freedom. Beyond this function of maintaining justice among individuals, "the state cannot do anything else without transgressing justice."

In his belief that the human race is improved by the dying out of the weak and unfit and the survival of the fit, Spencer objected to many government activities aimed at safeguarding the well-being of the individual as invasions on private liberty. These included state relief for the poor, state-financed education, governmental protection against fraudulent finance, any factory or sanitary legislation, and even a state post office. Every new act of legislation, in his opinion, stifles individual personal liberty.

For Spencer, as for Mill, the test of good conduct for an individual is whether that conduct brings him happiness and whether his actions further the happiness of other members of society. Spencer, also like Mill, admitted that doctrines, moral codes, in fact all ideas of good and evil vary from time to time and from place to place. In the past, he wrote, the great political superstition was the divine right of kings. What he and his contemporaries faced was superstition about the divine right of the parliament. The function of Mill's middle-class liberalism was to put a limit on the powers of the landed aristocracy that enjoyed a monopoly on political and social status and to curb legislation imposed by parliament on British society for the benefit of the upper class. The function of Spencer's liberalism was to put a limit to the powers of the parliament for any ends whatsoever.

The System of Party Government

The partisan creeds of liberalism and conservatism have played an important role in the history of the British parliamentary system. In the eighteenth century, the two opposing groups in the British Parliament were the Tories and the Whigs. The first favored the crown and represented the conservative landed aristocrats, great industrialists, and commercial creditors. In the era of Disraeli, his followers called themselves "young Tories," and ultraconservatives were referred to as Tories. The Whigs voiced the sentiments of the "middle class" merchants and indebted inland farmers.

In the nineteenth century, the Parliament witnessed the rise of two new parties—the Conservatives (who succeeded the Tories) and the Liberals (who succeeded the Whigs). Only in England, Scandinavia, and some of the British Commonwealth countries does a major national political party call itself "conservative." As the name of a political party, it appeared in England for the first time in 1830 alongside the other title, "Tory."

For the last half of the nineteenth century, political life in Great Britain centered around the names Disraeli and Gladstone. Benjamin Disraeli (who became Lord Beaconsfield) led the conservative forces for over thirty years. In an 1832 campaign speech, he said,

> "I am a Conservative to preserve all that is good in our constitution, a Radical to remove all that is bad. I seek to preserve property and to respect order, and I equally decry the appeal to the passions of the many or the prejudices of the few." (*Selected Speeches of the Late Right Honourable*

the Earl of Beaconsfield, Vol. I, ed. by T. E. Kebbel, 1882, p. 8.)

While he served as prime minister (1868; 1874-1880), Disraeli's foreign policy stressed imperialism, and he succeeded in expanding the system of England's interest and influence throughout the world.

The various groups which supported the parliamentary reform bill of 1832 gradually came together in the new Liberal Party inspired by the philosophy of Mill. It stood for free trade, an enlarged suffrage, removal of the political disabilities of Catholics, Jews, and dissenters, and the worldwide abolition of serfdom and slavery. In addition to abolishing slavery in all British territories, the Liberals initiated extensive social legislation (the "Factory Acts" and others) and laid the foundations of a modern civil service.

The most prominent leaders of the Liberal Party in the nineteenth century were Lord John Russell, Lord Palmerston, and William E. Gladstone. Gladstone, who was prime minister four times in the period of 1868 to 1894, has come to symbolize the British Liberal heritage in the mind of posterity. Moral ideas carried enormous weight for Gladstone—the two greatest influences on his thinking were his Christian religion and Mill's political philosophy. He assumed God to be on his side. His daily prayer times, morning and evening, were rigorously observed, and he read a sermon of his own composition to his servants each week. Gladstone's faith kept him from being a whole-hearted utilitarian, but he relied very heavily on Mill's economic theories.

Although Gladstone had reservations about income taxes in principle, his political skills ensured that Britain had a progressive income tax long before Germany, France, or the United States. He succeeded in molding British opinion to accept social reforms that culminated in old-age pensions and other welfare legislation. The economic policies he instituted, including free trade, brought balance and equilibrium to the British nation, while other countries underwent many upheavals. Historian Eugenio F. Biagini writes that "as a great charismatic leader, Gladstone was able to square the circle of making classical liberalism viable in a mass democracy." (*Liberty, Retrenchment and Reform: Popular Liberalism in the Age of Gladstone, 1860–1880*, Cambridge University Press, 1992, p. 4.)

In the Gladstonian period, the motto of the Liberal Party was "Peace, Retrenchment, Reform." It was Sir Henry Campbell-Bannerman, who became Liberal prime minister in 1905, who first introduced the phrase "the British Commonwealth," to imply a more liberal, democratic entity than did "the British Empire." Under the rule of the Liberal Party, a comprehensive program of social reform was inaugurated, including progressive taxation.

During World War I, David Lloyd George, the leader of the Liberal Party, formed a coalition cabinet which survived the first election after the war but was overthrown in 1922. Sharp differences between the remedies offered by different factions within the party to solve the nation's postwar problems disintegrated the Liberal Party, and its radical members joined the Labor Party.

Representatives of trade unions and socialist groups who were elected to Parliament had formed the Labor party in 1900, with the election of 1906 making Labor's first major impact in Parliament (fifty members). Throughout the years, it increased its representation, and following the 1922 election, it became the official opposition. Its program was aimed at alleviating unemployment and at numerous internal improvement projects.

The two principal parties in Great Britain today are the Conservative Party (which like the Tories appeals to the gentry and the upper middle class) and the Labor Party (which appeals to organized labor and the lower middle class). Among the minor third parties which may on occasion hold the balance of power is the small Liberal Democratic Party formed in recent years, which in name only recalls the powerful Liberal Party of former years.

In the United States in 1872, a short-lived Liberal Republican Party was formed to oppose Grant's first administration. Its aims were civil service reform and reconciliation with a South still suffering from the Reconstruction. A convention held in Cincinnati named Horace Greeley for President, but he was defeated by Grant in the presidential election. With

Grant's overwhelming victory, the party lost its reason for existence.

Many early American leaders profoundly distrusted the party system. For John Adams, our first Vice President and second President, the division of the republic into two great parties was "to be feared as the greatest political evil under the Constitution." The frequent splits and subsequent formation of new parties increased misgivings about a party system. In spite of the fact that the Founding Fathers looked with mistrust at the party system, the United States evolved a working system of party government.

Traditional and Modern Forms of Liberalism and Conservatism

Approaching the beginning of the twenty-first century, we may ask: What are the functions of liberalism and conservatism in the last decades of the twentieth century? The term "liberal" in its present sense appeared in American political history at the close of the 1930s. The American idea of liberalism—at that time—was a far cry from the English liberalism of the nineteenth century. Liberal American intellectuals of the period (for some obscure reasons "intellectual" became synonymous with "liberal") applauded the recognition of the Soviet Union and supported the Loyalists in the Civil War in Spain. Some outspoken liberals justly or unjustly became unpopular with their fellow citizens as pro-Soviet fellow-travelers, or antireligious secularists.

Closer to our own times, so-called liberal ideas—for instance, that the government must provide security "from the cradle to the grave" and that it owes its citizens a living instead of giving them the opportunity to achieve one—remain unpopular with those who believe that the government must give its citizens the freedom to earn and to provide for their own needs.

The traditional and radical concepts of Mill's and Spencer's liberalism are now regarded as "right wing" conservative viewpoints. Those who hold these views tend to dismiss all modern liberals as "extreme left radicals." At present, we can hardly witness a political campaign without a candidate being labeled by his opponent— disparagingly—as a "liberal." In American politics the word "liberal" has, at least in some circles, become a pejorative term. This contempt is expressed even more strongly when a political opponent is described as "a liberal with a capital L" or as "an egg-head left-wing liberal," whose political program is "to tax and spend."

Why does present-day liberalism not fit the original formulation of the meaning of that term as described above? Liberalism as originally conceived stressed the personal freedom of the individual and his right to dissent. It permitted governmental interference only to alleviate disharmonies created by individuals pursuing their own interests without regard to the interests of others. The reason that modern liberals are no longer identified with these beliefs may be found in the dramatic economic, political, social, intellectual, and ideological challenges that have occurred since the eighteenth and nineteenth centuries.

The Industrial Revolution, with its *laissez-faire* policies leading toward excessive individualism, deepened the poverty of the exploited masses. The growth of nationalism and the trend toward national self-determination seemed to be allied with the idea of individualism promoted by liberals, but in reality it strengthened the role of government—to mention only the iron rule of Bismarck in a newly united Germany. In our country, the response to the Great Depression of 1929 transformed the limited powers of the government into a kind of state paternalism, the purpose of which was to alleviate the devastating effects of the collapsing economy and the suffering caused by mass unemployment. The rise of imperialism and militarism led to two World Wars that resulted not only in massive loss of human life, but also in economic and political confusion that invited governmental action.

Conservatives, when that term was first used, looked with suspicion upon reforms (although Disraeli advocated profound ones). They feared revolutions as a breach of law and as destructive of the established existing order, an idea eloquently advanced by Edmund Burke in his *Reflections on the Revolution in France*. They wanted to preserve traditional values and did not approve of the concept of universal freedom and equality.

Charitable to those who need help, modern conservatives believe that an individual is responsible for his actions and that his rights are paired with responsibility. They accept changes only when they develop gradually from existing conditions without disrupting the continuity of society. History, however, shows that conservatives are able to overcome their instinctive resistance to change. For a long time, for instance, they were opposed to a conciliatory policy toward Red China. Yet it was the conservative President Richard M. Nixon who redirected the course of American diplomacy by establishing commercial and cultural intercourse between China and the United States.

It should be pointed out that since the early days of conservatism there has always been a profound difference between the American and British varieties. In Great Britain, class distinctions, recognizing differences of social origin, faith, and education, possessed an influential force in the hierarchical order surrounding society. In the United States, different values prevailed—respect for "self-made" men, for acquired possession rather than for inherited property, for the principle of democratic majority rule, for the inalienable rights of everybody in all areas of life, especially for every individual's right to equality of opportunity, which can lift men from "rags to riches," from the "log cabin to the White House." Because of these values, American conservatism was hardly a counterpart of British conservatism.

If by "conservative" we understand a person who emphasizes the importance of the past and opposes changes in old and established practices and usages, we can hardly find a modern American conservative who can claim adherence to traditional liberalism. In 1980 the promise of a return to the essence of traditional liberalism struck a responsive chord in the American voters attracted to Ronald Reagan. In his campaign, Governor Reagan stressed the evils of big government, advocated the liberation of the common man from governmental domination, and promised lower taxes and the restoration of the spirit of free enterprise.

In fact, during the years of the Reagan presidency, the nation faced increased spending on education, food stamps, and farm and other domestic programs. Instead of a balanced budget, the Reagan administration oversaw the largest increase in the national debt in the history of our nation.

The original concept of liberalism has become corrupted, whether it is claimed by modern liberals or conservatives. Liberalism, these days, is not so much a party creed as a philosophy that calls for a balance between the needs of the individual and the responsibility of the state in meeting such needs. For conservatives, the best government is the least government. For liberals, as Senator Hubert H. Humphrey once observed, "the true moral test of government is how it treats those in the dawn of life—the children; those who are in the twilight of life—the aged; and those who are in the shadow of life—the sick, the needy, the handicapped."

The conflict between modern liberals and conservatives does not, however, relate to care for children, the aged, the needy, or the handicapped. No one now questions the responsibility of the state for taking care of those who cannot help themselves. Today both conservatism and liberalism are dedicated to pursuing such programs as Social Security, Medicare, collective bargaining, bank deposit insurance, unemployment insurance, securities regulations, and agricultural price supports. Conservatives have not been able to offer constructive alternatives to these programs. The conflict arises when attempts are made to transform a government with limited powers into a paternalistic state, or when the state fails to alleviate disharmonies in society. It arises when the system of free markets, the tradition of incentives and rewards, and individuals' freedom of economic activity are undermined or straitjacketed.

Radical liberals' attempts to enact national legislation establishing compulsory unionism can serve as an example of the state's attempts to put legal curbs on the liberty of the individual. Such a legalized monopoly of all employment would violate a fundamental right of free citizens— the freedom of association, which includes the right not to join or to withdraw from any organization, including labor unions.

On the other hand, the issues of segregation and sex discrimination are examples of the state's failure to secure social justice until the ideas of modern liberals prevailed. Civil rights legislation ending racial segregation and guaranteeing equal employment opportunity took place during the liberal Kennedy and Johnson administrations. The liberals can claim that their compassion provided women and minorities the opportunity to lead fulfilling lives.

In the United States, liberalism and conservatism have never served as party creeds. We have liberal and conservative Democrats as well as liberal, moderate, and conservative Republicans. Neither of the major political parties has a doctrinaire set of principles that stand in fierce opposition to those of the other. The lines of distinction between the platforms of the two parties are not clearly drawn. There are no meaningful differences between the ultimate goals sought by the two parties. Instead the distinction lies in the role assigned by each of the parties to the government in achieving those goals. The Democrats have a tendency to use the government to furnish social services on a wider scale than the Republicans, who place greater faith in private initiative and in the individual's ability to shape his destiny.

One of the principal qualities of our party system, as in Great Britain, has been an atmosphere of mutual tolerance, resulting in the traditions of responsible opposition engaged in legitimate activity and of adherence to the rules of constitutional procedure and fairness. The spirit of political tolerance is sustained even in election years, when the political chips are piled high and campaigns tend to inflame the participants. No punitive action is taken by the winners against those who opposed them. Any attempt to transcend the bounds of what is legal, moral, and civil will turn the momentum in favor of the opposition.

A Liberal or a Conservative Church?

The atmosphere of mutual tolerance does not prevail, however, in all areas of our society's political and spiritual life. These days we hear, for instance, a great amount of talk condemning our ministers and church congregations for being too "liberal" or too "conservative."

It is not the purpose of this lecture to discuss the theological controversy between the "fundamentalists" and the "liberals." I shall only mention that the fundamentalists, who claim that they have the truth divinely bestowed upon them, see the Bible, the "dear old Book," differently from the liberals. They profess to believe in the Bible verbatim from cover to cover. For the liberals, the formative days of Christianity and of the Bible's origin are twenty centuries removed from the world we live in. To them, the Bible is just a priceless heritage of the past that requires interpretation to be applicable to the present. It should not, they maintain, be taken literally and cannot always be relied on to solve the problems of the twentieth century.

I wish to discuss, rather, the controversies of a political nature in which those who challenge the views of a particular group in the congregation are looked upon as giving aid and comfort to enemies who are labeled as "subversive liberals" or "reactionary conservatives."

The church's basic principles are obscured by a belief that some economic or political point of view is ordained by God and that adherence to that point of view is a test of loyalty to the church. These principles are further obscured when the churches are urged to discharge their responsibilities to society in accordance with politically liberal or conservative dogmas and not in the light of the teaching of the gospel.

Jesus was not a political leader. He offered his listeners no political advice but taught them the meaning of life and preached the purification of the mind and heart. He was, we may say, "liberal" in teaching that the Sabbath was made for man and not man for the Sabbath; he was "conservative" in reprimanding the Jews severely for their abuse of the laws and customs regulating divorce. Neither did the Apostles take sides in solving the political problems of their day.

Christian philosophy, which cannot be neatly labeled as either liberal or conservative, has exerted a strong influence on our sense of social responsibility. Christianity's belief in the worth and dignity of every individual has prompted many beneficial reforms and created new opportunities for the underprivileged. For example, the abuses that characterized the Industrial Revolution—such as brutal contempt for human life and the exploitation of men, women, and children—are only a memory now. They were abolished by social legislation that provides for numerous public services and environmental planning. Education has become general, and the development of individuals' spiritual lives has been kept relatively free of political implication. By no stretch of the imagination is God's will done in all areas of our lives; yet we have been richly endowed.

The gospel, concerned as it is with all human activities, seeks to create conditions which secure freedom and well-being for all people—the strong and the weak, the talented and the handicapped. Persons are not to be regarded as economically expendable commodities. It is the sacred obligation of every person to enable others to live in decency. Does this mean that the "welfare state" should be advanced as the sole expression of moral consciousness? Not at all. Christianity refuses to endorse a materialism that debases the soul, but it also strongly repudiates state interference that denies individual liberty.

The ethical precepts given by Christ have an eternal quality which, unlike economic or political doctrines, cannot be limited to a certain time or place. Christianity never has been a stagnant pool but a river flowing constantly onward. Its ethic is dynamic. It modifies the spirit and the will of man, and it possesses regenerative and redemptive qualities that cannot be contained by either a liberal or a conservative framework.

God's unique design for mankind, as opposed to that which He has for all other creatures, is the power to choose between good and evil. The power of choice—an essential part of conscience—vests in human beings a sense of personal responsibility for the results of their choices. "One man esteems one day as better than another, while another man esteems all days alike. Let every one be fully convinced in his own mind." (Romans 14:5.)

Some sincere members of a congregation may see in liberals' programs that stress the role of the state in securing the well-being for all men a road to justice; others may see the ideal of maximum individual freedom from state control advocated by conservatives as the road to prosperous society. Since there is no particular economic or political system ordained by God, the church should leave the creation of new economic and political initiatives and the displacement of others to other structures and to individuals.

When Christianity attempts to gain secular power by merging with the state or a political party, it ceases to be Christianity. Parties with a high-sounding religious emphasis do not always follow in everyday politics the generally accepted ethical demands of the church. Although they may claim to be aimed at application of Christian principles to practical political life, often they prove to be as susceptible to abuse as all other parties are.

In Austria prior to World War II, for instance, the Christian Socialist Party under the leadership of Engelbert Dollfuss (later assassinated by the Nazis) attempted to organize a Catholic proclerical dictatorship. The parliament was suspended, political parties dissolved, and freedom of press and assembly abolished. Leaders of the opposition were arrested, their headquarters raided, and civilians with firearms executed. When the socialists barricaded themselves in some of the municipal housing projects, Dollfuss did not hesitate to bombard the workers' apartment blocks with artillery. Having replaced all political parties by creating the so-called Fatherland Front of 1934, Dollfuss issued a new constitution. The preamble of the new 1934 constitution proclaimed: "In the name of Almighty God from Whom all law emanates, the Austrian people receive this constitution of its Christian, German, Federal State based on the corporative principle." The name "Christian" as used by the party in power was harshly abused.

In Germany, in order to "coordinate" the twenty-nine self-governing major Protestant churches, the National Socialist Party advocated the unification of the established churches into one national church subordinated to the state. The Nazi protestants organized into a group known as "German Christians" and saw no basic conflict between Christianity and National Socialism. They called themselves the "storm troopers of Jesus Christ," and their target was the destruction of the dignity of the individual with the cruelty that marked the darkest pages in the modern history of mankind.

The postwar period marked the increased influence of Christian Democratic Parties in Italy, France, and Germany. It is a misconception, however, to assume that the Christian Democratic Parties monopolized the best hopes of the church. Like any other political party, a Christian party is engaged in political warfare. Within the party, a struggle for influence is continually taking place among the various groups. Indeed, the name "Christian" may be meaningless in identifying the political goals of a party that uses this name.

The prime objective of the ministry of the churches is to deal with the ultimate issues of man's life, namely, faith, conscience, and salvation. Faith is the source of freedom. Attitudes which grow out of faith may be summarized in Martin Luther's two formulae: A Christian is the perfectly free lord of all, subject to no one else; a Christian is the perfectly free servant of all, subject to everyone, accountable to God. "None of us lives to himself, and none of us dies to himself." (Romans 14:7.)

Liberalism and Conservatism in the Administration of Justice

One of the healthy manifestations of our democratic system is the nonpartisan administration of justice. There seems to recur, however, a tendency from time to time to appoint Supreme Court justices based on their political ideology rather than on their knowledge, experience, and prominence as jurists. This tendency was recently clearly demonstrated by President Bush's nomination of Clarence Thomas as the "best qualified man," although the forty-three-year-old nominee had only one year of judicial experience. The nomination was motivated by Thomas's public record of strongly conservative policy positions. He was confirmed by an exceptionally close Senate vote (52 to 48). To no one's surprise, Justice Thomas has maintained a high level of agreement with his most conservative colleagues (Justices William Rehnquist and Antonin Scalia), thus justifying the hopes conservative political circles placed in him.

From such circles, one also hears disappointment about and criticism of Supreme Court justices who in their decisions do not adhere to the principles of the presidents who appointed them. Chief Justice Earl Warren, a "disobedient" Republican appointee, did not vindicate the hopes of conservatives during the Eisenhower administration. Recently the Republican appointees of the Reagan and Bush administrations, Sandra Day O'Connor, David Souter, and

Anthony Kennedy, have been accused in conservative circles of forming a new "moderate" coalition "emerging to block the high court's alleged conservatism." (Paul A. Gigot, "Mea Culpa: Souter May Be Bush's Blackmun," *The Wall Street Journal*, July 2, 1993, p. A6.) The three justices joined the decision not to overrule *Roe v. Wade*, thus helping to defeat the Bush administration's effort to overturn this decision, which established a constitutional right to abortion. Together with Justices Harry Blackmun and John Paul Stevens, they formed a five-to-four majority that reaffirmed a narrowed version of the *Roe* ruling and prohibited states from banning abortion altogether.

As I have pointed out, the meanings of the terms "liberal" and "conservative" have varied over the years. At present they have been defined in an arbitrary way by politicians and social commentators. Whether one is "liberal" or "conservative" according to their labels depends on one's attitudes toward labor matters, civil rights, and governmental economic regulations. In regard to the administration of justice, "liberal" judges, as the label is used, tend to extend the scope of civil rights laws and of economic entitlements and to protect the economic interests of working people, while "conservative" judges tend to uphold legislation that benefits the business world and to limit the extent of civil rights legislation.

The conventional political labels—such as "right-ward leaning conservative," "moderate conservative," "moderate liberal," "centrist" or "neoliberal," and "radical"—can be misleading when applied to the members of the judicial branch. The question of the liberalism or conservatism of Justices Byron White and Harry Blackmun proves this point.

Justice White, a Democrat appointed by President John F. Kennedy in 1962, was described as "conservative" at the time of his retirement in 1993. In the course of his career, he was "liberal" as an ardent supporter of civil rights and of federally imposed school desegregation, but he was "conservative" in opposing a broad use of quotas and of expansive racial preferences in employment policies (such as some affirmative action remedies for past discrimination). He joined the "conservative" judges in his dissenting opinions in cases involving abortion and in cases creating controversial new protection for criminal defendants.

In his dissent in the case of *Roe v. Wade*, Justice White wrote, "I find nothing in the language or history of the Constitution to support the Court's judgments. The Court simply fashions and announces a new constitutional right for pregnant women and, with scarcely any reason or authority for its action, invests that right with sufficient substance to override most existing state abortion statutes." (93 S.Ct. 762, 763 [1973].) He believed that the legislative branch of government should enact new laws rather than the courts' engaging in the creation of new constitutional rights. In the *Bowers v. Hardwick* case, Justice White pointed out the limited role that the courts should play. In the majority opinion that upheld a Georgia antisodomy law, he wrote: "The Court is most vulnerable and comes nearest to illegitimacy when it deals with judge-made constitutional law having little or no cognizable roots in the language or design of the Constitution." (106 S.Ct. 2841, 2846 [1986].)

President Nixon, who nominated Justice Blackmun, described him as a "strict constructionist" and "the Minnesota Twin" of "conservative" Chief Justice Warren Burger. It turned out that Justice Blackmun, who was expected to serve as a "conservative" balancing vote within the "liberal" Burger court, wrote the opinion in the *Roe v. Wade* case that guaranteed a woman's access to abortion. With this landmark opinion he created a judicial legacy that has had a lasting impact not only on privacy rights and civil rights within the field of constitutional law, but also on political life. (It should be mentioned that although the *Roe* decision is often identified with Justice Blackmun, it was arrived at by a seven-to-two vote.)

Justice Blackmun, who retired in 1994, did demonstrate some conservative leanings in the fields of business and criminal law, but he gained a reputation as a "liberal" voice in the Court by voting with the "liberal" Justices William Brennan and Thurgood Marshall on civil rights cases. In a 1991 television interview, Justice Blackmun declared, "Republicans think I'm a traitor and Democrats don't trust me. So I twist in the wind, owing allegiance to no one, which is precisely where I want to be."

Were Justices White and Blackmun liberal or conservative? Did Chief Justice William Rehnquist betray the conservative cause when he stunned prolifers by delivering the opinion in *Madsen V. Women's Health Center* that sustained an injunction barring prolife protesters within thirty-six feet of a Florida abortion clinic? In addition to the thirty-six-foot "taboo zone" established in the original injunction, a Circuit Court judge had forbidden protesters to approach patients or employees within a 300-foot radius unless invited and drew a similarly large protective circle around the houses of the clinic's staff. The Supreme Court objected to the 300-foot prohibitions but allowed the thirty-six-foot zone, which Chief Justice Rehnquist in the majority opinion said "burdens no more speech than necessary to accomplish the governmental interest at stake." (129 L.Ed.2nd 593, 611 [1994].) This decision was severely criticized by Justice Antonin Scalia. Tolerating such an injunction, he argued, turned the First Amendment into a victim of the prochoice position.

Do we expect a person who is politically active to remain an activist on the bench? Justices should not bow to political pressures. As Chief Justice Hughes stated in the *Macintosh* case: "But, in the forum of conscience, duty to a moral power higher than the state has always been maintained." (51 S.Ct. 570, 578 [1930].) To paraphrase this statement, we can say that, in the forum of conscience, duty to a moral power is higher than the loyalty to the political party that nominated the justice.

The prominent American jurist John Forrest Dillon (1831-1914) once stated, "*Ethical* consideration can no more be excluded from administration of justice, which is the end and purpose of all civil laws, than one can exclude the vital air from this room and live." On a similar note, Justice Felix Frankfurter explained that the administration of justice is based upon the conscience of society, ascertained as best may be by a tribunal disciplined for the task and "environed by the best safeguards and *disinterestedness* and *detachment.*" (Emphasis added.)

The administration of justice should be based on disinterested ethical considerations detached from "conservative" or "liberal" dogmas. Although the history of presidential appointments shows that political considerations have played an important role, I hope that the time will never come in this country when—as under totalitarian regimes—the courts become instruments of the ruling party and the administration of justice is subordinated to the political end of assuring the continued authority of the party in power.

I am reminded of the well known passage in one of Justice Cardozo's lectures. The judge, he said,

> "is not a knight-errant, roaming at will in pursuit of his own ideal of beauty or of goodness. He is to draw his inspiration from consecrated princi-

ples. He is not to yield to spasmodic sentiment, to vague and unregulated benevolence. He is to exercise a discretion informed by tradition, methodized by analogy, disciplined by system, and subordinated to 'the primordial necessity of order in the social life.' Wide enough in all conscience is the field of discretion that remains." (Cardozo, *The Nature of the Judicial Process*, Lecture IV, p. 141 [1921].)

Conclusion

Finally, let me reiterate that liberalism has had a rich and ever-changing history. John Stuart Mill represented the strict interpretation of classical liberal concepts; the freedom of the individual to pursue his own interest was the hallmark of his liberalism. With the rise of social reforms and increased governmental activities in the fields of social welfare and economic life, some tried to identify liberalism with socialism or, often, to disguise socialism as liberalism. There is a great dissimilarity, however, between these two doctrines. Karl Marx projected the future as an eternal conflict between classes, with industrial society tending to form a new nation of the proletariat, uniting workers throughout the world. Mill's dream was a natural harmony created by the individual's right to pursue his own interests (with certain limits to avoid injustice). The state's role was only to alleviate peripheral disharmonies that might create insecurity and distress. In meeting the realities of modern life, we may find a need for the government to secure through legislation equality of opportunity. But for liberalism to survive it must always stress the crucial elements of individualism—personal freedom and the right to dissent.

Conservatives see history as a continuum and wish to preserve for posterity the spiritual and political standards and principles inherited from past generations that have demonstrated their value and importance in the course of human experience. The basis of these standards and principles was to give the individual an opportunity to pursue his own interests and to prevent the usurpation of authority by the central government. These standards and principles, conservatives maintain, cannot be replaced by a belief that a strong government can bring justice and prosperity to all men. This belief, as the experiences of countries under totalitarian regimes demonstrate, is founded on a delusion that causes pain when faced with reality.

Reality, however, also does not permit us to ignore the dramatic changes that have taken place since Mill announced his basic liberal concepts now characteristic of conservative beliefs. The rise of social reforms resulted in a similar rise of governmental responsibilities and commitments for social improvement.

The tensions between liberals and conservatives can be alleviated if reason is not subordinated to emotion. Although they may not share the same political views, liberals and conservatives must claim the Constitution as their common basis. Reason guided the writers of the Constitution when they emphasized the importance of checks and balances and established a government divided into three branches to prevent centralization of political authority. In accordance with the spirit of the Constitution, government officials are not masters but public servants. Their duty is to protect the individual's equality of opportunity and to undergird him in his efforts to obtain a decent standard of living.

Reality does not permit us to ignore the profound changes that have occurred in the last century involving a growing role for government in meeting the needs of an urban, industrialized, and economically interdependent society. Change is the law of life, and such change requires many adjustments to ensure that the new needs meet with a sense of responsibility to our fellowman consistent with the moral requirements dictated by the community in a given stage of its development.

Finally, reality does not permit us to ignore the fact that, as Thomas Jefferson pointed out, there are two natural parties of mankind:

> "Men by their constitution are naturally divided into two parties. I. Those who fear and distrust the people, and wish to draw all powers from them into the hands of the higher classes. 2ndly, those who identify themselves with the people, have confidence in them, cherish and consider

them as the most honest and safe, altho' not the most wise, depository of the public interest. In every country these two parties exist, and in every one where they are free to think, speak, and write, they will declare themselves. Call them therefore liberals and serviles, Jacobins and Ultras, whigs and tories, republicans and federalists, aristocrats and democrats or by whatever name you please, they are the same parties still, and pursue the same object." (Letter to Henry Lee, August 10, 1824, *Basic Writings of Thomas Jefferson*, ed. by Philip S. Foner, Willey Book Company, 1944, p. 800.)

It is harmful to the nation when political leaders, satisfied in their own doctrinaire righteousness, close their eyes and ears to the nation's needs that do not fit into the framework of their dogmas. The existence of the two "natural parties" pointed out by Jefferson stresses the importance of political dialogue, guided by moral idealism, between those holding opposite views. Unless politics is undergirded by moral idealism, it is a betrayal of responsible citizenship.

DEMOCRATIC VALUES AND CAPITALIST EFFICIENCY: THE LIBERAL RECONCILIATION

by

James Tobin

James Tobin

James Tobin is Sterling Professor of Economics Emeritus at Yale University. He has been on the Yale faculty since 1950. He retired from his teaching position in 1988.

Professor Tobin was graduated from Harvard College summa cum laude *in economics in 1939. He received a Ph.D. in economics from Harvard in 1947 and was a Junior Fellow of the Society of Fellows for three years, 1947-50, the last of which he spent at the Department of Applied Economics at the University of Cambridge, England.*

In 1961-62, on leave from Yale, he was a member of President Kennedy's Council of Economic Advisers in Washington. He was President of the Econometric Society in 1958, of the American Economic Association in 1971, and of the Eastern Economics Association in 1977. In 1955, the American Economic Association awarded him the John Bates Clark Medal, given to one economist under age 40. He has been a member of the National Academy of Sciences since 1972.

In 1983, Professor Tobin received in Stockholm the Prize in Economic Science, established by the Bank of Sweden in memory of Alfred Nobel.

He is author or editor of thirteen books and more than three hundred articles. His main professional subjects have been macroeconomics, monetary theory and policy, fiscal policy and public finance, consumption and saving, unemployment and inflation, portfolio theory and asset markets, and econometrics. He has written both for professional readers and for the general public.

DEMOCRATIC VALUES AND CAPITALIST EFFICIENCY: THE LIBERAL RECONCILIATION

by

James Tobin

Economic Inequality, Endemic to Capitalism

Democracies treat their individual members as equals, equals before the law, equals in voting and other political rights. Yet capitalist markets generate serious inequalities, reflecting inevitable differences in the earning capacities of individuals, in their efforts, ambitions, and habits, and in sheer luck. The efficiency of capitalist markets in generating progress in living standards for entire peoples depends on innovation and competition. Change brings losers as well as winners, and painful insecurity. How can the egalitarian principles of democracy be reconciled with the inevitable economic inequalities of capitalism? This is perhaps the pervasive underlying issue of political economy in our capitalist democracies.

Historically, many reformers have sought to democratize the workplace itself, giving workers control of enterprises and enabling them to share its fruits. But for economies to be efficient, enterprises have to be subject to the disciplines of competition, including possible bankruptcies and deaths. Whether owned by workers or by capitalists, these institutions cannot be guaranteed immortality or protected from competition without fatally impairing the efficiency of a market economy.

To realize an efficient allocation of workers among occupations and enterprises, it is essential that individuals of different skills earn different wages. It is not feasible to set egalitarian wages by law, or to adjust employees' wages fully to their families' needs and responsibilities.

In the useful categories suggested by Albert Hirschman, business enterprises are "exit" institutions, while governments are "voice" institutions. For "exit" institutions, what is important is the availability of alternative choices, not voice in governance. Shoppers and employees who retain the right to exit at will can scarcely claim the right to participate in control. In contrast, individuals have much less choice of the political community of which they are members and, as such, subject to its laws and policies. "Exit," if possible at all, is costly, and there are few alternative choices available. As citizens, their only way to exert their will is by "voice", which in principle in a democracy is distributed equally.

We need not push the distinction to extremes. There are, after all, numerous ways in which workers, under the protection of labor laws, participate in making enterprise policies: collective bargaining, coparticipation, profit-sharing. There are also numerous governmental regulations governing industrial relations: minimum wages, limitations of hours of work, severance regulations, health and safety requirements. Capitalism has survived most of these interventions, although not without costs and inflexibilities.

Capitalist enterprises will inevitably generate quite unequal incomes among the individuals who own them and work for them. Market-generated economic inequalities are likely to offend the egalitarian ethics of democracy, The remedy must be sought in governmental policies—not so much in modifying the incomes that enterprises and markets generate in the first instance as by altering disposable incomes by taxes and transfers. Such redistribution is the subject of this lecture.

Conservatives, Liberals, and Redistributions

Probably the biggest issue between conservatives and liberals is the use of state fiscal and regulatory powers to redistribute income and wealth in order to diminish economic and social inequality. In particular, should the structure of fiscal transfers and taxes be progressive, subsidizing the poor and burdening taxpayers more than in proportion to their income or wealth?

One's answer to this question has to be a balance of two considerations. One is the inherent desirability of a less unequal distribution than is generated by capitalist economic activities and markets. What is fair? What is just? These are matters of values, individual and social. They cannot be wholly determined by reason and fact.

In saying that views of economic justice represent subjective values rather than objective truths, I am consciously giving short shrift to attempts, whether as ancient as Plato or as recent as Rawls (*A Theory of Justice*, Harvard University Press, 1972), to deduce rules of economic justice from first principles. Rawls' maximin criterion (maximize the consumption of the least fortunate member of society), for example, has no compelling intuitive appeal to me. I doubt that the "haves" of contemporary society would find convincing the contention that they voted for redistribution in a constitutional convention held before they were born and before the random drawing of endowments of human capital and other wealth in which they were so fortunate.

Suppose, to take an artificial and extreme example, that the random draw gave 100 of the 1,100 members of a community living standards of $1,000, and the other 1,000 members living standards of $10. In the best of circumstances, the Rawls' criterion would reduce by 90 percent the incomes of the one hundred fortunate persons, raising the poorer thousand to the mean income of $100. Raising the less fortunate group just to $60 would cost the minority only 50 percent. Yet one might, like Rawls, vote for full equalization on egalitarian grounds, given that redistribution is costless in aggregate output.

However, suppose each one percentage point in the levy on the fortunate hundred has a Laffer-curve disincentive effect, reducing the pre-tax production and income of the rich by 1 percent. A tax of 85 percent would be needed to equalize disposable incomes of everyone at $22.80. But full equality would not meet the Rawls criterion; it does not maximize the least disposable income, once the disincentive costs of taxation are recognized. A 50 percent tax would leave mean disposable income higher, at $54.40, the two groups at $250 and $35, still unequal but better in dollars for both groups than the equality outcomes and better by my reckoning of values too.

This is indeed the Rawls solution, because no higher or lower tax rate will make the disposable income of the poor higher than $35 per person. This is also the top of the Laffer curve, the tax rate that yields the most revenue. Although it is presumably Rawls' choice, it is probably not a utilitarian's choice. A tax rate of 40 percent, for example, would lower the per capita disposable income of the poor only from $35 to $34, while raising that of the rich to $360, mostly because the lower tax induces them to produce $600 instead of $500. If one values the consumption of the rich positively at all, one might find such a trade-off worthwhile. But continuing on that line makes each increment of rich consumption less valuable to society and each decrement of poor consumption more costly.

(Let ry and py be rich pre-tax and poor pre-transfer incomes per capita respectively, and ryd, pyd be their disposable (after-tax and -transfer) incomes. Let x be the rate of tax on the rich, and tr by the per capita transfer to the poor. ryd = (1-x)ry; pyd = py + tr = 10 + tr. First, assume no discentive effects of taxation. ry = 1000; tr = 100x. Equality means (1-x)1000 = 10 + 100x, thus x = 0.9. Mean y and yd are always 100, and aggregate yd is 110,000. Second, assume disincentives such that ry = (1-x)1000, thus rdy = $(1\text{-}x)^2 1000$, tr = 100x(1-x) and pyd = 10+100x(1-x). It follows that pyd is maximized when x(1-x) is maximized, at x = 0.5. Setting pyd and ryd equal and solving the resulting quadratic equation for x between 0 and 1 gives the result in the text. Aggregate yd declines from $110,000 for x = 0 by $10,000 for each tenth of a point of tax.)

The example introduces the second of the two considerations, the cost of reducing inequality, in terms of the economic well-being of society as a whole and of the persons whose welfare suffers in the process. One might regard redistribution as desirable but find that the cost of bringing it about is too great. There is a trade-off between efficiency, in the sense of maximum social production, and the mitigation of inequality in its distribution. Unlike attitudes towards economic justice, the costs of redistribution are in principle amenable to reasoned analysis and factual research.

Both elements in this trade-off are, in general, relevant to a decision on the big issue of policy. It's not decisive to point out the injustices of the economic outcomes of capitalist markets, without considering the costs of remedying them. Neither is it decisive to point out that there are social costs in redistributive policies, without also arguing that the costs outweigh the benefits of greater equality.

Transfers and taxes are two sides of the same coin. Taxes are payments of individuals to governments for which the individual receives no specific service in return. Transfers are payments of government to individuals for which the recipients render no specific service in return. Transfers must be distinguished from government purchases of goods and services. These purchases are sometimes called "exhaustive" expenditures, because they are public drafts on the productive resources of the economy. When governments run schools and universities, for example, they employ manpower, use land and buildings, and buy supplies, which might otherwise have been available for private use. Transfers from taxpayers to other private citizens are, in contrast, not exhaustive; they do not absorb productive resources for governmental use. Rather, they shift command over those resources from some private parties to others. The distinction is important but should not be pushed too far. Because of disincentive effects, transfers may indirectly diminish the gross domestic product (GDP) available to the society as a whole. And many substantive government purchases may, like public education, also have distributive consequences.

Prior to the welfare state the distributive aspect of fiscal policy was confined to the distribution of the burden of the taxes needed to finance public exhaustive expenditures. Redistributive possibilities were enormously magnified by the advent of transfer programs for social insurance and welfare.

We would agree, I suppose, that the inequality of concern to us is that of *life-time* income and consumption *within* a birth cohort, not of annual or monthly or daily income. Purely age-related differences of income, which do not alter lifetime incomes, do not call for correction by taxation or transfer. The fact that fifty-year-old men systematically earn more than twenty-year-olds and seventy-year-olds is not an inequity. The twenty-year-old can look forward to being fifty, and the fifty-year-old must anticipate declines as he adds twenty years to his life. Likewise, individuals' incomes vary randomly from year to year, but tend to regress so that this year's unlucky are likely to be lucky in future years. Chronic inequalities are a much bigger problem than reversible inequalities.

Measuring Your Personal Redistribution Tolerance Coefficient

The late Arthur Okun in his marvelous Godkin Lectures, *Equality and Efficiency: The Big Tradeoff* (Brookings Institution, 1975), concocted a parable to measure one's willingness to see an economy give up consumption in aggregate in order to spread it more evenly. It goes something like this—I take the liberty to paraphrase. In the freezer of the royal palace of an oil-rich Middle-East country is stored a massive stockpile of ice cream for the delectation of the king, his family, and the wealthy elite of the capital. Fifty miles across the hot desert are poor nomads. There is no way to deliver ice cream from the palace to them without losing some fraction of it to the heat of the sun.

Here is the test question by which can be determined your Redistribution Tolerance Coefficient (RTC): What is the largest fraction of melting loss you would tolerate and still regard as worthwhile a transfer of ice cream from the palace to the nomads? There is, of course, no right answer to this question. An exceptionally hard-hearted conservative would answer "zero." At the other extreme, the caricature of a soft-hearted liberal would answer "99.6 percent." Try the test on your friends or your students. You will find the answers very revealing.

We could make the RTC test question more relevant to the United States today; for example: What fractional loss of GDP would you tolerate in order to reduce the prevalence of poverty, as officially defined, from 15 percent of the population to 10 percent?

The Okun parable is a prototype of the issues involved in much of the contemporary debate about social and economic policy. Virtually all programs to benefit the poorer and less advantaged members of society do involve some costs, like the melting of the ice cream in transit. These are typically the consequences of disincentives to work or to save or to take risks on the behavior of the more affluent taxpayers who finance transfers to the poor and on the behavior of the recipients themselves.

Hard-hearted conservatives and soft-hearted liberals usually disagree about the magnitude of these disincentives and costs. The conservatives say that the costs of "welfare" transfers, for example, are very high relative to the gains actually realized by the intended beneficiaries and by society at large. The liberals say that the conservatives' favorite tax reforms, like cutting taxes of capital gains, will result in minimal gains to the economy as a whole but in substantial windfalls to the wealthy at the expense of poorer citizens.

These are differences of opinion about facts. Unfortunately economics and other social sciences, lacking the opportunity to make decisive controlled experiments, while they can narrow the range of legitimate disagreements, can seldom resolve such disagreements definitively.

Even if agreement on the factual side of the Big Trade-off could be achieved, there would remain basic disagreements on the values, as revealed by the diverse measures of the RTC elicited by the Okun test. Those disagreements are the true stuff of politics and ideology. I remember a group of undergraduates who asked me to discuss this subject with them. One of them asked me if I didn't believe in the Tenth Commandment. For him, that clinched the matter—redistribution was stealing. For others, the obvious presumption was for strict equality.

Why Reduction of Inequality Is Desirable

I offer my own opinion on the values side of the tradeoff. In theoretical models of general economic equilibrium, individuals have exogenous "endowments" of commodities, including talents and skills. Whether genetic or environmental, these are the basic sources of economic welfare and of inequality. Suppose it were feasible to reduce by taxes and transfers the inequalities of original endowments, *in ways that would not themselves affect their allocation among different uses*. Specifically, no one, rich or poor, would change behavior—for example, substitute leisure for the consumption afforded by paid employment—simply because of taxes and transfers. Society would reap the benefits of the talents of Michael Jordan or Bill Gates or the Beatles without enriching them so extravagantly. Would any one oppose such redistributions on principle?

I can imagine some grounds for opposition, although I don't find them attractive. One argument is that some people are better utility machines than others ("utility" is the economists' word for satisfaction, gratification, or enjoyment). Even if interpersonal utility comparisons were meaningful, we have no reason to believe that the capacity for enjoyment is positively correlated with initial endowments. That may be true of particular commodities and activities. Some of us may have a comparative advantage in appreciation of art or music—but across the board, a generic capacity to love life?!

I think Abba Lerner (*The Economics of Control*, MacMillan, 1946, pp. 29–32) was right. Human beings are human beings; at least that is the faith underlying our modern democratic societies. We do not ascribe social and economic status by caste or class or race or sex. Lacking any other basis for assessing capacity to enjoy life, we must assume it is randomly distributed, independently of endowments. This provides a Bayesian probabilistic presumption for equality. Any other assumption would founder not only on the uncertainty of measurement but on the obvious self-interest every individual would have to claim and display more utility potential than his neighbor.

Sources of Inequality, Personal and Circumstantial

If we agree so far, then we agree that the failure to equalize resource endowments, by taxation or otherwise, is *instrumentally* justified, but only instrumentally justified. We don't know how to equalize without inducing tax-reducing or tax-avoiding and transfer-increasing behavior, which deprives both society and government treasuries of some of the potential productivity of the nation's resources. If we could assess the value of every individual's native talent in its most productive use and tax her, positively or negatively, on that basis, she could not escape by loafing instead of working, taking comfortable jobs instead of responsible ones, consuming instead of saving, hoarding instead of risk-taking, imitating instead of innovating. Human endowments, like land, would be assessed and taxed at the value of their highest use. For better or worse, this cannot be done. (In the case of real property taxes, an ingenious device for eliciting realistic self-assessments is to require the taxpayer to accept any offer to buy the property at whatever price he declares for tax calculations, but this cannot be done for human talent.)

Society necessarily taxes the individual outcomes of endowments-cum-behavior, not of endowments alone. It's pretty clear that many controversies arise from differences of emphasis as between the two components. Advocates of equalization usually attribute observed inequality mainly to endowments, and opponents emphasize the role of behavior. These differences affect judgments both about "justice" and about "social efficiency."

We can, I suppose, imagine an economy of disjoint individual economies, with Robinson Crusoes of equal endowments of physical and human nature, each satisfying all his needs from his own effort and ingenuity, without specialization or trade or cooperation. It will then seem unjust and inefficient to tax the industrious and ingenious in favor of the lazy and improvident. However, even these Crusoes may be subject to chance fortunes and misfortunes, due to weather and health and technology. They may wish to join each other in an insurance scheme, even though the inevitable moral hazard imposes some deadweight loss and injustice. The moral hazard arises from the impossibility of distinguishing losses due to chance from those due to the behavior of the insured.

But endowments are not equal, and individual economies are not independent. Even if endowments were initially equal, they would not remain so in the next generation. The children of successful, industrious, fortunate, wealthy parents have a head start. Others start with immense handicaps.

The inequality of children's starts in life presents a great dilemma. A proud claim of our casteless democratic society is equality of opportunity. This presumed equality is our excuse and consolation for inequality of economic outcomes. The prizes may be unequal, but we like to think that after all they are won in a fair race. Embracing equality of opportunity, conservatives scorn liberals for wanting governments to tackle inequalities of economic outcomes and conditions. But if the starting advantages in the next race are correlated with the order of finish of the last one, is opportunity truly equal? Is the race really fair? We can only hope to mitigate the problem by a progressive tax-transfer system, including inheritance levies, and by public education.

A work ethic is essential to a society. We have a great stake in maintaining the view that performance pays off, that indolence and inefficiency do not. Since we cannot disentangle the elements of endowment and chance and effort in performance, we must tolerate considerable rewards for genetic endowment and luck, rewards in large measure undeserved and redundant.

The interdependence of modern economic life makes it difficult to attribute any person's economic success or failure wholly to the person's own efforts and merits. After all, this is not a society of isolated subsistence farmers. Anyone's earning capacity is dependent on a complex web of relationships—on economic, locational, and professional specialization and trade; on a highly developed legal and governmental system that enforces contracts, protects life and property, and fosters markets; and on a shared accumulation of culture, learning, science, and technology. Market prices are usually a good way of allocating resources, even when the competitive conditions that would justify identifying factor prices with marginal productivities only approximately obtain. What is not justified is the presumption that these prices or marginal productivities are just deserts. It is not unreasonable to attribute part of the national product to general societal overhead capital and to allocate it as a social dividend for equal division.

How much inequality can a democratic society—or any society, for that matter—stand before the legal, social, and political foundations of its economic productivity are undermined? These foundations depend on consent, expressed not only in formal collective political action but in the informal daily actions of individuals and groups. A complex, interdependent market economy is extremely vulnerable to disaffection. It is a great illusion to rely solely on legal compulsion to sustain the rules of the economic game—to protect every property, enforce every contract. As Weber, Schumpeter, and other thoughtful analysts of the sociology of capitalism long ago pointed out, the framework must be sustained by a widely shared and internalized ethic, an ethic that deviates from feudal explanations of inequality precisely in *not* ascribing differences of income and power to differential birth rights. It is too much to expect that loyal consent to the rules of the game will be forthcoming regardless of the outcomes of the game and regardless of perceptions and suspicions that the game isn't really fair. We don't know the extent to which the disquieting problems of crime, corruption, demoralization, and antisocial behavior which beset cities in America and elsewhere are due to extreme and highly visible—probably more so than ever, thanks to television—differences of opportunity and quality of life. It would be imprudent, to say the least, to ignore the possible connection and to rely wholly on police and prison.

Conservatives sometimes argue that individuals who have a taste for reduction of social inequality should contribute generously to private charities rather than advocating state measures to force others to pay taxes to finance redistribution. The trouble is the so-called "isolation paradox." You as an individual might favor redistribution and be willing to pay taxes for the purpose. Yet you know that your own voluntary contribution of the same amount would not achieve meaningful social results. You are willing to contribute if other people will also, but not on your own.

Confronting the Big Equality/Efficiency Trade-off

I return now to the trade-off between the egalitarian gains of redistributive fiscal policies and the losses due to the disincentives of taxes and transfers. This is a matter on which utilitarian calculus can conceivably shed some light, although for the reasons I gave at the beginning, it can never be conclusive. Unfortunately our empirical knowledge of the strength of the disincentives is terribly thin.

Even a voter who places no social value on the utility of those above him in the income scale will not rationally favor taxation to bring them all the way down to his level. There is a point beyond which higher surtax rates collect less revenue, not more. Arthur Laffer was right on this point, even if he vastly exaggerated it for political and ideological effect. If majority voter–taxpayers pushed surtaxes on wealthier citizens beyond this point, they would have to impose more taxes on themselves. This is because high surtaxes would induce wealthier citizens to divert resources to leisure or other untaxed uses of time and money.

The presumption that the marginal utility of consumption declines as an individual's level of consumption increases is the reason for believing that, other things equal, transfer from richer to poorer increases total welfare, the more so the greater their differences in consumption and the steeper the marginal utility curve. Taxes are the least costly to society if they can be levied on taxpayers whose economic activity is relatively insensitive to changes in disposable income and wealth. These principles, with assumptions about the relevant marginal utilities and behavioral elasticities, can be used to construct an optimal tax and transfer structure, but it is a complex calculation.

The optimum will generally be progressive and will include a positive per capita "demogrant"—a guaranteed minimum disposable income for anyone with zero earnings, which serves as a refundable credit against taxes for anyone with positive earnings. If there are some individuals with zero or near-zero endowments, and if their corresponding marginal utilities of consumption approach infinity as their endowments approach zero, then any utilitarian calculation which includes them will dictate a positive demogrant. Although this will require higher marginal tax rates for more fortunate citizens, utility losses on this account will be balanced by the gains at the bottom.

In the United States, we have been struggling to dodge this problem for decades, hoping to avoid the budgetary costs of a universal demogrant by restricting transfer payments to citizens who can be observed or reasonably inferred to have zero or minimal endowments. "Categorical" systems of this type inevitably run into formidable problems of inequity and disincentive. Trying to save taxpayers' money by making sure that only households below the poverty line receive "welfare" destroys incentives to work. You lose all benefits once your earnings take you across the arbitrary poverty threshold. Similarly, confining benefits to the category of single-parent families impairs incentives to form and maintain two-parent families. The opportunities for innocuous, fair, and cost-saving categorical discrimination are quite limited.

The utilitarian approach to optimal taxation implies that, contrary to the premise of many writings, ethical principles and interpersonal valuations, although necessary, are not sufficient to determine the shape of the optimal tax schedule, even in general terms. The schedule also depends on the behavioral responses to taxes and transfers because these determine the costs that must be weighed against the utility gains of redistribution. These will differ as between economies, and for the same economy at different times. For example, the costs of redistribution will be higher the larger the taxes that must be levied for the substantive programs of government.

Following these lines of inquiry, economists have been making important contributions to this subject. (See J. A. Mirrlees, "An Exploration in the Theory of Optimum Income Taxation," *Review of Economic Studies*, April 1971, pp. 175–208; A. B. Atkinson, "How Progressive Should Income Tax Be?" Association of University Teachers and Economics *Proceedings*, and A. B. Atkinson and J. G. Stiglitz, *Public Finance*.)

Limiting the Domain of Inequality

American attitudes toward economic inequality are complex. Our society accepts and even approves a large measure of inequality, even of inherited inequality. Americans commonly perceive differences of wealth and income as earned and regard the differential rewards of effort, skill, foresight, and enterprise as deserved. Even prizes of sheer luck cause little resentment. People are more concerned with the legitimacy, legality, and fairness of large gains than with their sheer size. These attitudes are probably associated with Americans' hope that their children and grandchildren, if not they themselves, will be successful and affluent.

But willingness to accept inequality in general is tempered by a persistent strain of *specific egalitarianism*. This is the view that certain commodities should be distributed equally, or at least less unequally than the ability to pay for them. Candidates for such sentiments include basic necessities of life, health, and citizenship.

Our institutions and policies displace or modify market mechanisms in many cases. Contracts by which people sell themselves into slavery are forbidden, and so are sales and purchases of votes. Although Civil War draftees were allowed to transfer obligations for military service to others, along with monetary payments, that market has been illegal in this century.

Of current topical interest is the widespread view that access to basic medical care should be universally available, independent both of individuals' ability to pay for it and of their probabilities of needing it. By the same token, society does not want the beneficiaries of subsidized health care to contrive in any way to cash it in and use the proceeds for other purposes. Likewise society intends by giving the poor food stamps, housing vouchers, and free schooling instead of cash, to redistribute nutrition, shelter, and education, not liquid fungible income.

Cannot certain crucial commodities be distributed less unequally than the market would distribute them, given the inequality of income and wealth? The social conscience is more offended by severe inequality in nutrition and basic shelter, or in access to medical care or even legal assistance, than by inequalities in automobiles, books, clothes, furniture, boats, works of art, travel, and other luxuries. Can we somehow detach the necessities of life and health from the prizes that serve as incentives for economic activity, and let people strive and compete for nonessential amenities? I think this is a worthy goal.

Specific egalitarianism takes a number of different forms, with different motivations and rationalizations. As noted above, there are some "commodities" as to which strict equality is deemed so crucially important that society cannot permit an individual even voluntarily to transfer his or her shares to someone else. These include civil rights, privileges, and obligations, where equality among citizens is basic to the political constitution.

This category includes also biological and social necessities so scarce in aggregate supply that if they are unequally distributed by market processes some citizens will be consuming below a tolerable minimum. Distribution of scarce medicines, surgical procedures, and organ transplants is not left to the highest bidders. How about salvaging of prematurely born infants? Adoptions of children? Rentals of wombs or of ovaries?

At the other end of the spectrum are commodities of ample or potentially ample supply, where any egalitarian objective is not a strictly equal distribution but an assured universal minimum, a "safety net."

The elasticity of supply, short run and long run, is crucial. If government guarantees a basic package of medical insurance to everyone, should it forbid provision of extras to persons who can afford to and do choose to buy them with their own funds? Yes, for critical services that are in fixed short supply. No, if the services and the resources they require can be expanded in supply in response to extra demand. In the latter case, it makes no sense to deny cosmetic surgery to the rich if they prefer to use their wealth that way rather than buying a yacht.

Equity Across Generations

Issues of intergenerational equity have recently become prominent in several contexts. Are we shortchanging our descendants by leaving them a large government debt? By enjoying at their expense social security pensions that will not be available for them? By failing to leave for them sufficient stocks of productive capital and technological know-how to provide for them the living standards we enjoy? By using up exhaustible natural resources and irreversibly damaging the environment? By failing adequately to socialize and educate our children?

These are difficult questions, to which the answers are far from obvious. Tears for future generations may be misplaced or at least exaggerated. There is a good chance that, like ourselves, our children and our children's children will be the beneficiaries of scientific and technological innovations that will raise their life chances and standards of living far beyond those of preceding generations. If so, it is hard to make a case for the present generation to sacrifice in their behalf. It is especially hard to justify sacrifices by today's poor for the benefit of tomorrow's affluent. Yet that is precisely what many apostles of "generational equity" advocate when they propose as remedies curtailment of government social spending for disadvantaged families and children.

Whether government deficits and debt increase consumption today at the expense of consumption of future generations depends on the purposes of the public borrowing and the economic circumstance in which it takes place. Public investment in infrastructure, education, and environmental protection may frequently pay off sufficiently in higher consumption opportunities in future to justify borrowing private domestic saving and foreign saving to finance them. In periods of recession, financing government outlays by borrowing instead of taxes may be justified by the prospect that deficit spending will raise GDP, and increase productivity too. Frugality that results in recession and depression, unemployment and excess capacity, does not benefit our grandchildren.

Yet these considerations do not justify to younger generations and to future Americans the consumption binge afforded to the more affluent members of American society by the tax reductions and federal deficits of the 1980s. At last federal fiscal policy is forestalling further growth of public debt relative to U.S. GDP.

Inequalities Among Nations

The foregoing discussion refers to a democratic community, most likely to a single nation with a democratic central government. Can the same principles be extended to larger domains such as the European Union, perhaps—or indeed to the whole world? Certainly human beings everywhere have the same ethical importance as the citizens of the United States or of Italy or of the European Union as a whole. This is clearly a large and difficult subject, and it is beyond the ambition of this lecture.

In the absence of a democratic world community and a world government, there would be insuperable obstacles to a world system of taxes on and transfers to individuals. Clearly it will be a long time before migration across nations as free as migrations within nations will be possible. One prerequisite would be successful control of population growth in less developed countries.

Meanwhile, the wealthier nations of the world do have compelling obligations to help the billions of inhabitants of poor and underdeveloped countries. Experience suggests that assistance designed to place them on paths of self-sustaining development is more effective than simple additions to their consumption, except of course in famines and other crises. Experience also suggests that assistance to or through the nondemocratic governments of many poor countries often is of no help to sustained development or to the general populace. A country with a low per capita income has a reasonable claim for help from wealthy developed countries, but in many such countries there are ruling elites of great privilege and wealth. It is not reasonable to ask the median-income taxpayers of the United States to augment the incomes of people who are better off than they are, even though they reside in poor countries.

In these days the welfare state is unpopular, and indeed government itself is viewed with cynicism and anger. Americans are sure they are overtaxed. I have tried to remind you why there is a welfare state, why there is redistribution, why it is a function of democratic government, essential for democracy and capitalism to co-exist. There are, it must be remembered, more efficient and less efficient, indeed woefully inefficient, ways of economic management in general and of dealing with inequality in particular.

(For this lecture, I have drawn on previous writings of my own, in particular "Considerations regarding Taxation and Inequality", in Colin D. Campbell ed. *Income Redistribution*, American Enterprise Institute, 1977, pp. 127-134, reprinted in my *Policies for Prosperity*, Wheatsheaf, 1987, Chapter 42; and "On Limiting the Domain of Inequality," *Journal of Law and Economics*, Vol. XIII (2), October 1970, pp. 263-277, reprinted in my *Essays, Vol. 3, Theory & Policy*, M.I.T. Press, 1982, Chapter 25.)

THE INVISIBLE FOOT OF GOVERNMENT

by

Dick Armey

Dick Armey

Dick Armey is United States Representative for the 26th District of Texas. In 1994 he was elected to a sixth term and became Majority Leader of the House of Representatives.

Previously he was elected Chairman of the House Republican Conference, the third-ranking position in the House Republican leadership, for the 103rd Congress. With this win, he became the first Texan ever elected to the Republican leadership.

Congressman Armey received his undergraduate degree from Jamestown (North Dakota) College, his M.A. from the University of North Dakota, and his Ph.D. in Economics from the University of Oklahoma. Prior to his election to Congress, he was Chairman of the Economics Department at the University of North Texas.

As a member of the House leadership, Congressman Armey has the opportunity to help define the Republican agenda and restore his party's credibility on economic issues. He was named Ranking Republican on the Joint Economic Committee in early 1991 and served on the House Education and Labor Committee.

In 1988, Congress passed Armey-sponsored legislation to close obsolete military installations for the first time in more than a decade, saving taxpayers $2.3 billion annually. After finishing the base-closing battle, Congressmen Armey took the cause of modernizing American agricultural policy. In the midst of the 1990 budget summit, he led his House Republican colleagues in opposing the resulting tax and spending increases.

THE INVISIBLE FOOT OF GOVERNMENT

by

Dick Armey

It's a pleasure to be here. I have always been fascinated with this great University, built, as it was, from the top down, and I've had some association with the University over the years. Also, as some of you may know, my current occupation in life keeps me all too often in the relatively seamy world of politics. So to have received an invitation to speak on your campus on a subject that is something more than just sound bites is a welcome change for me.

I should tell you from the outset that I have no prepared text because, quite frankly, I've been too busy for the last few months to sit down and write anything. If the results of my discussion tonight are as rewarding as those that kept me from writing a prepared speech, I know *I*'ll have a good time.

Many of you are going to be struck by how bold I will be tonight. Many of you will disagree with what I say. Many of you will agree with what I say. Some of you will be offended by what I say. And some of you will be amazed that I dare to stand up in front of God and everybody and say it, but you will be secretly glad I did. Because I don't believe that when I have the extraordinary opportunity, as I do tonight, to speak seriously and thoughtfully about serious matters, that I ought to shrink from the task. Furthermore, there may be people here who can take what I have to say tonight and put it in a context that can bring harm to me personally in my professional life. But quite frankly, ladies and gentlemen, the right to speak freely of one's own mind and beliefs must be put ahead of personal and passing perils to one's occupation.

I will argue tonight that a conservative point of view is both morally and intellectually superior to a liberal point of view. This is not a thesis that one often finds expounded on college campuses. But I believe it profoundly. I am a professional economist by training and by trade and by self-definition. I am a politician by employment. I have let my economics define my politics, and I conclude that liberalism is both intellectually and morally deficient.

Now obviously as I discuss both these terms in such, shall we say, challenging language, I ought to be clear what it is I mean by liberalism and conservatism. I see conservatism as advocating more personal freedom and its attendant and mandatory responsibility and liberalism as advocating more government and its attendant dependency and irresponsibility.

In case you haven't detected this, I'm not a fan of big government. When it's necessary, government can be good. Government can be productive. Government can be helpful. But government inevitably will engage in excesses because it does not have the bridle of morality that is an essential part of freedom. Governments exist, for good or ill, for the purpose of making people do what they will not do voluntarily. In many instances, that is necessary, desirable, and productive of human well-being. But government is by definition rule by one person over another. I am not an anarchist because I do recognize that governments are necessary.

Anyone who would talk about these things must begin by explaining his own view of human nature. I believe human nature to be egocentric. Having grown up in the West, where folks are plain-spoken, I might have said "selfish" or "self-centered." But too many people might misunderstand; so I will use the word "egocentric." Human beings, then, are egocentric creatures, but we are also special creatures. We have a gift that God our Creator has given to no animal in existence. That is the gift of intelligence.

Man and man alone has the ability to understand, discover, and be creative with the wonders of the universe. It is my own view that God, like any good architect or engineer, was a mathematician, and that in fact he used calculus, and that is his greatest gift—I think any engineer alive today would validate that proposition. Nevertheless, there *is* an order in the universe, and we and we alone have the ability to comprehend it and to use it. Because we have intelligence, the ability to learn, to know that we were born, to know that we will die, to know that we have a heritage, and to know that we have a posterity—this makes us special.

We also have free will. We apply our free will against our egocentricity in one of two possible ways. If we are in touch with and governed by what I like to call the beautiful side of our egocentricity, then we are self-confident, we are humble, we are appreciative, we are dedicated to family, to country, to the well-being of other people. And if we are in touch with the dark side of our egocentrism, we are arrogant, we are selfish, we are greedy, we are chauvinistic, we are racist, we are nationalistic. I'm not going to touch on the question of whether this is determined by genetics or by culture—I don't want to wade into that debate—but I can tell you that I find the works of E.O. Wilson and his great book *On Human Nature* at the least entertaining and in fact informative and validating.

And so we must take a position on our egocentricity: Which will it be? As parents, we try to teach our children the rewards of walking on the beautiful side of egocentrism—how to love your country, how to love your children, how to love your nation, how to love your family, and how to love yourself. And as parents, we fear that our children will be governed by the other side. Each of us has both of these sides. I have told people for years that the most dangerous part of the human anatomy is the ego, and those people who allow themselves to be ruled by their ego are in their own lives and the lives of others very rarely productive.

So the question is how we meet our world, given our enormous and exceptional ability—with arrogance and pride or with respect and humility? I argue that we have, then, two great institutional frameworks within which we will carry out our communal relationships in life. One is freedom. The other is power. And the great institutions consist either in acts of freedom (free markets and free association) or in government (control, regulation, administration, and protection). These two institutions are inevitably and forever in competition with one another. The history of the world, especially the recent history of the world, validates my contention that in the end freedom will out. Certainly affairs in Eastern Europe have demonstrated freedom's power. But the lessons of freedom are always inconvenient and difficult to learn. The lessons of dependency, by contrast, are convenient, comforting, and easy to learn. This we see at our own expense as we teach our children. So the temptations in life are always on the side of power and government. And the struggle is always on the side of freedom.

What is a market? It is an arena for voluntary bilateral transactions between intelligent and free people. Now we concentrate most often, and certainly in my discipline, on the narrow area of how man provisions himself, on economic markets. But there is a market for ideas called the university. There is a market for spiritual enhancement called the church. There are many markets in the world. But in each you see voluntary associations between intelligent and free people, and make no mistake about it, what sets us apart is our intelligence. The least of us has a thousand times more intelligence than the brightest of God's dumb animals. And that is what makes us extraordinary and special.

I would argue that when we are in touch, and only if we are in touch, with the good side of our egocentrism, can we live in a world of voluntary associations. Character matters. Markets, if they are to work, must punish immorality. In order to illustrate this point and compare the functioning of a market with the functioning of the government, I draw on what is probably the most famous analogy ever in the history of economics. It is so famous that even historians and political scientists know it. That is Adam Smith's great analogy of the Invisible Hand of the Market, which was, of course, an analogy he presented, interestingly enough, in a treatise called *An Inquiry into the Nature and Causes of the Wealth of Nations* in the year 1776, which just happened to be the year of the birth of the world's greatest experiment in free society. In that book Smith talked about the self-centeredness of the butcher and the baker and the candlestick-maker and made the point that each pursued his own self-interest in all that he did. In doing so each was guided, as if by an invisible hand, to serve the needs of the community in a manner greater than ever he could if even he had aimed to pursue public good as opposed to private well-being.

Now many of us who cite the invisible hand of the market meet the contention that we merely have a "faith" in the market. I respond to that by quoting my hero, Thomas Sowell, whom I believe to be the smartest man alive in America today. When accused of having faith in the market, he said, "I don't have faith in the market; I have evidence." And so did Adam Smith have evidence: He was not writing a treatise on how the world should be. He was writing a treatise about the way the world was, by virtue of the evolution of behavior and the prosperity that followed when egocentric men followed their natural tendency to truck and barter. And he was demonstrating that freedom works.

Frederick Bastiat also made an important point, and one I think the current administration should pause to understand: that in a world of free associations and free markets and free people, it is the poor man who is able to benefit from the wealth of the rich man. He drinks the milk of the rich man's cows. He eats the fruits of the rich man's vineyards. He toils by virtue of his ability to be employed by the rich man. We do not have a zero sum society where one can only gain at the expense of the other, but in the free world there is a natural and necessary sharing of the wealth. The rich man can only succeed by sharing his good fortune with the poor man. And that is the beauty of the invisible hand of the marketplace.

Back when I was an academic, I got credit from my hero Milton Friedman for having created a corollary to the invisible hand of the market called the invisible foot of the government. I argue that when you have market competition—the only competition that rewards morality and punishes immorality, rewards winning and punishes losing, and always draws the best that we have to give and accepts nothing less than that—then the natural incentive system of the market mandates that we must each and every one of us rise with the greatest of our ability to whatever occasion may present itself. It is not only a result of the carrot of the invisible hand of the market, but also of the stick of the visible foot of the market.

That is why is it hard for us to see the goodness that comes from the free and mundane transactions of free people. It is always clear to us when there are people who lose and the market gives them a boot, after the fashion of Joseph Schumpeter's famous observation of "creative destruction." If you should take your time, your resources, your ability, your hopes, and your dreams and attach them to a venture for which your talents and skills are not suited, the market quickly gives you the message, "Get out of this business. You are losing money. You are going broke. You are not suited to this business." A business failure is the exception, but the exception that stands out like a sore thumb.

The visible foot of the market is also very honest. If you engage in business in a dishonorable way, if you lie, steal, or cheat in a world of voluntary transactions, you will be quickly found out, and intelligent people will not willingly do business with you. The market punishes immorality with certainty and swiftness. And so the visible foot of the market that Schumpeter called creative destruction (and notice he never said it was destruction, but *creative* destruction) kicks you out of this activity or reforms your behavior in order to take the resources that you would command unproductively or immorally and put them into the hands of someone who would use them productively or morally because Schumpeter knew very well that the scarcity of the market can never allocate "to" unless it allocates "from." That is why he chose the word "creative."

Only in the market do we have a set of natural incentives that accommodates to the best side of our egocentrism, our desire to succeed. As we worry about our earning more or doing more, we end up doing right by being efficient, by using all the virtues.

Now, unhappily, my political economy has a more complete anatomy than just the market. Over on the left side of my political economy there is the *visible* hand of the government. The government inevitably holds out its hand to the losers. Our government today, more than ever before in our history, is engaged primarily in the transfer of income from those who have to those who do not. And what you find in government programs, instead of market competition, with all its incentives that require excellence and morality, is a political competition that has ample incentives for inefficiency and immorality. That is the visible hand of the government.

We see the government, for example, holding out its hand to an American peanut farmer and saying to him, "We will give you a card"—a card like this one, embedded with a computer chip—"and by virtue of the right granted by your government with this card, you shall have the extraordinary privilege of selling peanuts in the American economy for the consumption of your fellow citizens." And we all say, "Isn't that good?"

Ah, but on the other side, on the right side of our political economy, there is something called the invisible foot of the government. By virtue of extending the privilege to sell peanuts for domestic consumption to those precious few, the federal government kicks around every other possible potential grower and seller of peanuts and says, "You are not allowed, you are disallowed from engaging in that activity, irrespective of your personal morality, your standing in the community, your work ethic, or the quality of your natural resources. We decide you are not allowed." But no one sees that. We only see the visible hand of the government taking care of the poor peanut farmer. And, I daresay, if you can find a poor peanut farmer, please show him to me.

The peanut farmer now, because he has a government program, finds that his ability to get a loan at the bank is greater than the cotton farmer's (who has a government program too, but not one quite so reliable as the peanut farmer's, though certainly a better program than the soybean farmer's).

And so we see in our political anatomy that what the government does is say to people that if you lose, you win; if you win, you lose. If you are moral, you are disqualified, but if you are immoral, we are indifferent to that question.

What we end up with, then, is a competition between two institutions. Those of us who believe in individual abilities and individual integrities and the functioning of a free community's free exchange in providing a moral society carry on a debate with those who think we must have government regulation because, it is alleged, people are unable to care for themselves.

Now I will argue with you that if you look at this political economy and only see the visible left side of it, you will see the visible foot of the market and fear the market, and you will see the visible hand of the government and adore the government. And you will be a liberal. A liberal does not see good happening unless he sees the government do the good.

Recently a prominent public figure lamented over our current health care system, and I quote, "There isn't a *system*. What you have is millions of people doing millions of different things." Now, what kind of a system allows millions of people to do millions of different things? None. What she was observing was not a system at all, but rather freedom, the absence of government control. This public figure was exasperated by a lack of control.

What she could not see is that the best of what happens today in America is invisible. It is so ordinary, we don't notice it.

Now, if you strain your imagination and try to see the full anatomy of the political economy, you will see, in addition to the left side that is visible, the right side that is invisible. You will see the glorious morality and generosity of the market, and you will see the inglorious mean-spiritedness of the government.

It is on this basis that I come to the conclusion with which I began—that a free society will always be morally and intellectually superior to a society that places its confidence in government. I would further argue that not only will it be a morally and intellectually superior, but also a more prosperous, society. Because in taking its precious resources and allocating them among competing ends, a free society will get greater output, and each individual in the society will enjoy a growing and greater share of an ever-increasing pie. It will be a society free enough to allow people to discover all those millions of new and different things that all those millions of different people can do. Each of those millions of individuals will do what no amount of government control could ever do for him—realize his unique, God-given potential in ways that widen the circle of happiness for all. This is the morality of markets.

In summation, let me just leave you with this sound bite, which I call Armey's Axiom No. 1: The market's rational, the government's dumb.

FROM PUBLIC WELFARE TO PRIVATE VIRTUE: SHIFTING LIBERAL AND CONSERVATIVE CONCEPTS OF SOCIAL WELL-BEING

by

Edward J. Harpham

Edward J. Harpham

Edward J. Harpham is Associate Professor of Government and Political Economy at The University of Texas at Dallas. He earned his B.A. in Political Science from the Pennsylvania State University in 1973, and his M.A. and Ph.D. in Government from Cornell University in 1976 and 1980, respectively.

Following a year as a resident fellow at The Institute for Humane Studies in Menlo Park, California, Professor Harpham taught in the political science program at the University of Houston from 1978-81. He joined the faculty at The University of Texas at Dallas in the fall of 1981. From 1986-89, Professor Harpham was College Master in the School of Social Sciences. He was elected Vice President of the Southwestern Political Science Association for the academic year 1993-94.

Professor Harpham's research focuses upon the role that economic ideas have played in the shaping of modern political thought and the making of public policy. Along with numerous articles, he is the co-author of a book on the history of political science and the editor of three books on public policy. His most recent edited book is John Locke's Two Treatises of Government: New Interpretations. *He is currently working on two major research projects: a study of the political and economic thought of Adam Smith and an analysis of the relationship between long-term economic development and political change in America.*

FROM PUBLIC WELFARE TO PRIVATE VIRTUE: SHIFTING LIBERAL AND CONSERVATIVE CONCEPTS OF SOCIAL WELL-BEING

by

Edward J. Harpham

I

The recent election provides entertaining material for beginning an essay on liberalism and conservatism. Democrats and Republicans alike spoke about "kicking the crooks out of Washington." The problem facing the electorate was deciding which party was to be the kicker and which the kickee. It was a tough decision.

Democrats enjoyed an open season on conservative ideas for most of the summer. Conservatism, they told us, was a four-letter word with twelve letters. They claimed that conservatives were running in circles trying to get us back to where we once were. How prophetic! What the Democrats didn't know, of course, was that where we were going in the 1994 election was back to 1952, the last time the Republicans controlled both houses of Congress. To be sure, there were subtle differences between 1994 and 1952. After all, one would never have mistaken Bill for Ike, would one?

Republicans were little better in their characterization of their liberal opponents. Nothing captures their postelection disdain for liberalism more succinctly than the famous quip by Benjamin Disraeli, "Anyone who is not a liberal when he is young has no heart; but anyone who is not a conservative when he is older has no mind."

My concern in this essay is not with what liberals or conservatives think about each other. But rather to inquire into how each thinks about social well-being in America today. Even a cursory reading of the history of political thought teaches us that there are many different ways for thinking about what it means for a society to prosper. As Michael Walzer reminds us in *Spheres of Justice* (Basic Books, 1984), medieval societies looked at the problem of social well-being quite differently than we do today. For people of the medieval world, an undeniable dimension of social well-being was the creation of good Christians. The condition of one's soul was a public problem demanding the ongoing attention of the state. Personal health, on the other hand, was considered to be a private affair, best left in the hands of the individual.

In this essay, I will examine two distinct concepts of social well-being found in contemporary political debates. The first, a modern liberal concept, views social well-being largely in material terms: A society is prosperous to the degree to which its members have more material resources available to use as they see fit and these resources are distributed equitably among all people. To accomplish the twin goals of material prosperity and equity demands a strong and expansive state apparatus. Indeed, from the modern liberal perspective, the fundamental problem facing policy makers is figuring out how the state should intervene in the economy to provide the maximum welfare benefit to the most people at the minimum cost.

The second concept of social well-being to be discussed might be broadly characterized as "modern conservative." Like the modern liberal, the modern conservative sees material well-being as a crucial component of social well-being. The conservative, however, is suspicious of the liberal concern over economic equity. From this perspective, the very institutions built over the past fifty years to assure economic equality are seen as destroying the moral fiber of the nation. What sort of individuals are being created by the state? What must be done to our nation's welfare institutions to assure the production of a virtuous rather than a dependent population? How do we create a moral citizenry in an advanced industrial economy? The issue of private virtue has come to lie at the heart of this second concept of social well-being.

Critically examining liberal and conservative concepts of social well-being is an important undertaking. I am convinced that current debates over controversial policy issues are being driven in large part by shifting notions of what social well-being is all about. We are in the midst of a great reevaluation of the public philosophy. The liberal ideas which have directed the nation for the last fifty years are being challenged by new conservative ones. By better understanding the clash between liberal and conservative concepts of social well-being, I believe we can gain a useful insight into where we have been in the past, what we are about in the present, and the prospects and possibilities we face in the future.

II

The modern liberal concept of social well-being developed in response to the economic changes introduced into American society during the Roaring Twenties, a period best characterized by Joseph Schumpeter's notion of creative destruction. Innovative technological complexes were driving rapid economic growth and creating a new social order. At the same time, they were destroying an old one. Industries built around automobile production, electricity, radios, and motion pictures turned America into the first industrial economy geared to the production of durable goods and cultural fare for the masses. Between 1921 and 1929, annual automobile sales rose from 1.5 million vehicles to 5 million. By the end of the decade, car ownership was extended to 60 percent of all American families, and 40 percent of all American families owned radios. America had been remade in a new modern image. (See B.

Berry, E. Harpham, and E. Elliott, "Long Swings in American Inequality," *Papers in Regional Science*, Vol. 74, No. 2, 1995.)

The government's role during the economic boom of the 1920s was a far cry from the activist role envisioned by Progressive intellectuals since the turn of the century. As Calvin Coolidge put it, "The chief business of the American people is business." The purpose of government was not so much to curtail or check the abuses of capitalism as it was to unleash free market forces to serve the community as a whole. Fueled by the tax cuts and probusiness initiatives of the Harding and Coolidge administrations, the economy in the 1920s seemed to reaffirm the traditional promise of American life: Limited government plus a free market economy would inevitably lead to unimaginable material prosperity. Growth was not only natural, it was expected. As the economy grew, society and its members would prosper. Between 1922 and 1928, the real gross national product increased nearly 40 percent and real disposable per capita income rose by over 23 percent.

There was, however, another side to the economic boom of the 1920s. As in other periods of technological transformation and creative destruction, most notably the 1820s and the late 1860s to early 1870s, income inequality grew quickly. Between 1922 and 1928, the national income received by the wealthiest 1 percent of the population rose from 15.58 percent to 17.18 percent. While the real wages of urban skilled workers rose by 11 percent, that of unskilled workers fell to 1915 levels before returning to their 1920 peak in the 1927. Similarly, as the lower 93 percent of the nonfarm population saw its average real disposable income per capita fall by 4 percent between 1923 and 1929, that of the top 1 percent of the nonfarm population increased by 63 percent. But the real losers during the economic boom of the 1920s were the farmers. Rapidly expanding productivity brought on by technological innovations coupled to stagnant markets led to market gluts and declining prices, driving many farm families into bankruptcy. By 1929, the average per capita farm income was only 36 percent of the average per capita nonfarm income. (See Berry, Harpham, and Elliott, 1995.)

Various efforts were made by the Harding and Coolidge administrations to address the plight of the farmers. Tariffs were used to protect agriculture from overseas competition. Agricultural cooperatives were promoted as a way to self-organize the industry. However, the Republican administrations refused to pass legislation that would provide large scale farm relief. Along with other losers in the new American economy, farmers were left on their own to deal with the gale wind forces of creative destruction.

The economic boom of the 1920s came to an end in the summer of 1929 as the economy began to sour. Following a brief recovery in the winter of 1930, the economy began a downward spiral: Real per capita GNP fell by 10.9 percent in 1930, another 8.4 percent in 1931, 15.4 percent in 1932, and 2.4 percent in 1933. Meanwhile, unemployment rose from 1.6 million people in 1929 to 12.8 million in 1933. At the depths of the depression, one quarter of the work force was unemployed. By the end, one out of every eight farmers had been driven off his land. (Donald R. McCoy, *Coming of Age: The United States during the 1920s and 1930s*, Penguin Books, 1973, p. 178.)

The election of Franklin Roosevelt offered Americans a striking alternative to Republican rule. Early New Deal legislation such as the Agricultural Adjustment Act, the Civilian Conservation Corps, and the Federal Emergency Relief Act provided immediate aid to those whom the depression had harmed the most. Other legislation such as the Glass Steagal Bank Act and the National Industrial Recovery Act sought to bring stability to an economy that had experienced a banking crisis and a period of ravaging deflation brought on by the misguided policies of the Federal Reserve Board.

Later New Deal legislation sought to assist in a more systematic way those who had lost the most during the 1920s. The Social Security Act helped to establish a state/federal unemployment insurance system and a number of state/federal welfare programs to assist dependent children, the elderly poor, and the blind. It also put into place a new national old age insurance program for the elderly funded by payroll taxes. Along with other later New Deal legislation such as the Wagner Act (which established a National labor Relations Board), the Agricultural Adjustment Act of 1938 (which provided cash subsidies for farmers who curtailed production and practiced soil conservation), and the Civil Aeronautics Acts (which cartelized the airlines industry under state control), the Social Security Act laid the foundations for the state institutions and interest group politics that would define American political life for the next fifty years.

Taken as a whole, the New Deal articulated a new liberal vision about what social well-being meant in America and how it was to be achieved. It reaffirmed the belief that the promise of American life lay in material well-being. But it added to this a commitment to economic equity. People were better off to the degree to which they had more wealth to spend. But this wealth had to be distributed more fairly than the capitalist economy appeared to be able to do on its own. Technological innovation carried in its wake tremendous social upheaval and dislocation that were no longer politically acceptable. The state had a positive duty to bring stability, order, and equity to the capitalist process of creative destruction.

The triumph of this liberal concept of social well-being can be seen along a variety of dimensions. Statistically, it can be captured best in terms of a changing distribution of wealth. As a result of the New Deal, there was a significant decline in inequality. The disposable income of the top one percent of the population fell from an 18.9 percent share in 1929 to 7.7 percent in 1946,as the share of the top 5 percent fell from 33.8 percent to 17.7 percent. At the same time real family incomes of the upper 20 percent of the population went up 26 percent and the real wages of unskilled urban workers increased by 53 percent. (See J. Williamson "American Prices and Urban Inequality Since 1920," *Journal of Economic History*, Vol. 36, pp. 304-333; and S. Lee and P. Passell, *A New Economic View of American History*, Norton, 1979.) Many explanations have been offered for this "distributional revolution," including progressive taxation, the demographic movement away from agriculture, and the rise of organized labor. Whatever the proximate cause of this redistribution, the undeniable fact remained that America had moved in a more egalitarian direction in a relatively short period of time. This distributional pattern would continue to hold into the 1980s, when new inequality would emerge out of yet another wave of technological transformation.

Statistics on diminishing inequality in America are only part of the story. A second indication of the triumph of the liberal concept of social well-being can be seen in the vast expansion of the American state over the next fifty years. The New Deal was only the beginning, laying the groundwork for initiatives in regulatory and welfare policy that sought to build a set of state institutions that could provide material prosperity to portions of the population while guaranteeing a certain level of equality in society as a whole. The most successful example in this regard was the pension program we have come to call Social Security.

The origins of America's social security system lie in the Social Security Act of 1935. The Old Age Survivors Insurance Program was originally conceived as a social insurance program funded through payroll taxes. Unlike traditional welfare programs, social insurance was based on the idea that one acquired rights to benefits provided by the program based upon one's ongoing contributions. The more one "contributed" to the program, the more benefits one could expect in return upon retirement. By demanding that the program be self-supporting, Roosevelt believed that the program would contain built-in safeguards that would secure its financial stability over the long run. (See E. Harpham, "Fiscal Crisis and Social Security Reform" in A. Champagne and E. Harpham, eds., *The Attack on the Welfare State*, Waveland Press, 1984.)

Thus, in the beginning, the social security pension system sought to secure one pillar of the liberal vision of social well-being—material prosperity for the elderly. Old Age Survivors Insurance was an alternative to the more radical egalitarian proposal by the Townsend Movement, a group which sought a flat pension of $200 per month for all retired people. But egalitarian concerns did not remain in the background for long. Congressional debates over what to do with a growing trust fund culminated in the passage of the Social Security Amendments of 1939, legislation that would forever change the scope and direction of the federally sponsored pension system. Under the Amendments, supplemental benefits were provided for dependents and survivors of covered workers. The benefit starting date was advanced until 1940, and, in a significant modification, benefit rates became based upon monthly wages rather than cumulative wages. In short, egalitarian concerns over the needs of individuals had compromised the original social insurance goal of basing the program upon the idea of rights earned through one's contributions.

On a practical level, the 1939 Amendments undercut the financial safeguards built into the original program. Initially, the social security pension system was to be self-funded. Workers' payroll tax contributions would accumulate into a large trust fund which would be drawn upon when the workers retired. The 1939 Amendments not only provided benefits up front to individuals who had not contributed a corresponding amount to the trust fund, but they delayed implementation of payroll tax increases that were needed to maintain the long-term solvency of the program under its original specifications. Not until 1950 was a new linkage forged between contributions and benefits, one that provided a tremendous stimulus to the realization of the liberal vision of social well-being in the lives of almost all Americans.

The 1950 Amendments to the Social Security Act put into place what we now know as the "pay-as-you-go" system. The major features of this system are well known: The taxes of current workers pay for the benefits of current retirees. Future benefit payouts will be funded by future tax increases. In effect, there was to be a social contract across generations that would be enforced by the government. It would be a contract everyone could be expected to buy into because everyone would benefit from it either indirectly when his parents retired, or directly when he retired.

Pay-as-you-go was an ideal programmatic vehicle for developing an expanding institution embodying a liberal vision of social well-being. Start-up costs were relatively low because of the high ratio of workers paying taxes into the program to retirees collecting benefits. In the early years of the program, a small increase in taxes or expansion of active workers covered by social security could translate into a sizable benefit increase. The net effect of the pay-as-you-go mechanism was to depoliticize, for the most part, the entire question of social security. Throughout the 1950s and 1960s, few politicians were willing to challenge the wisdom of expanding either the coverage (that is, those workers who were mandated by law to participate in the program) or the benefits provided by the state-sponsored program. By providing generous benefits under supposedly conservative financial auspices, social security bridged partisan conflict and enabled everyone to buy into the liberal vision of social well-being.

The high watermark of social security expansion took place during the Johnson and Nixon administrations. A flat monthly benefit to begin at the age of seventy-two was passed in 1966. Significant benefit and tax increases were put into effect in 1967. During the War on Poverty years, tax contributions rose from $16 billion in 1965 to $30.1 billion in 1970, and benefits rose from $16.7 billion to $28.8 billion. But this expansion paled in many ways to that which took place during the Nixon years. Not only were benefits increased significantly in the late 1960s and early 1970s, but in 1972 the program was indexed to the rate of inflation. The goal of indexing was clearly stated in a report released in 1971 by the Advisory Council on Social Security:

> "Social Security beneficiaries ought to be able to count on the continued purchasing power of their benefits. These groups are among the least able to bear the brunt of inflation, and they should not be forced to reduce their levels of living, which tend to be minimum levels because of the lags that accompany ad hoc adjustments."

In effect, indexing permanently guaranteed to retirees the liberal promise of American life regarding material well-being. No longer would the purchasing power of benefit checks be subject to an uncertain economic climate or the whims of the political process. The state would secure in an equitable manner the economic well-being of all who came under its umbrella and do it in a relatively nonpolitical manner.

The dominance of a liberal concept of social well-being extended far beyond politics and policy-making into the world of ideas. During the 1960s and 1970s, numerous academics and journalists came to look upon the expansion of state institutions in the twentieth century through the lens of a liberal concept of social well-being. In study after study from this period, we find Whiggish-like histories describe the struggle and triumph of state institutions over the instabilities and inequities fostered by the capitalist economy. (See, for example, H. Wilensky and C. Lebeaux, *Industrial Society and Social Welfare*, Russell Sage Foundation, 1958; T. H. Marshall, *Class, Citizenship, and Social Development: Essays*, Greenwood Press, 1963/73; and N. Furniss and T. Tilton, *The Case for the Welfare State*, Indiana University Press, 1977.)

The broad outlines of the liberal model of the institutional development of the modern state are familiar to many of us today. Following the economic depression of the early 1890s, this interpretation would argue, populist pressures mounted for more progovernment involvement in the economy. Unbridled economic competition was perceived to be a threat not only to selected interests in the economy but to democratic life itself. The regulatory reforms of the progressive era represented the initial triumph of a progovernment perspective that sought to moderate the excesses of dangerous brands of competition. These reforms, however, were cut short by the "return to normalcy" of the 1920s. Unfortunately, the prosperity brought on by the return was an unnatural, unstable condition, fed by speculative profits and greed. The stock market crash and the Great Depression which followed were the inevitable result of a capitalist economy, geared to serving the few, that had gone out of control. Roosevelt's New Deal represented the triumph of the forces of good democracy over the darker forces of capitalist economic life. There was more left to be done, more problems to be dealt with, more constituents to be served than even Roosevelt imagined. In this view, the War on Poverty, Civil Rights legislation, and the regulatory initiatives put into place in the 1960s signaled a new era in American political life when the liberal promise of social well-being articulated first during the New Deal could be more fully realized. The conclusion about American political life which followed from such histories was powerful: The continued expansion of the state's institutions and powers was both inevitable and desirable. For American society to prosper, the reach of the state's regulatory and redistributive powers must be extended to all aspects of American life.

At the same time that this new Whiggish history of the American state was being written, liberal political philosophers began to rethink the whole question of what constituted social well-being and how our ideas about it could be used to evaluate social, political, and economic institutions. Well into the 1960s, the dominant popular and intellectual defense of the liberal concept of social well-being could be broadly characterized as utilitarian: A society was considered to be just when its major institutions were arranged so as to achieve the greatest balance of satisfactions when summed over all its members. (See J. Rawls, *A Theory of Justice*, Belknap Press, 1971, pp. 22-27; and A. Sen, *Inequality Reexamined*, Harvard University Press, 1992, Chapter 5.) The primary role of the state thus was to assure through public policy the creation of a just or, at least, a more just society. However noncontroversial the utilitarian defense of the liberal concept of social well-being might be to a person in the street or a politician supporting the expansion of social security, it raised some difficult philosophical questions. One of the most troubling of all was that of interpersonal comparisons of utility. How was it possible to calculate social well-being across individuals if we have no way to compare the well-being of one individual with another? Should all satisfactions experienced by individuals be accounted for in the social calculus, or just legitimate ones? Does redistributing a dollar from a rich person to a poor one make society better off? Isn't it just as likely that the psychological pain suffered by a rich person in losing a dollar outweighs the happiness of the poor person in being given a dollar? To put the question slightly differently, what is the relationship between individual well-being and social well-being?

Through a series of articles written in the 1950s and 1960s and his 1971 book entitled *A Theory of Justice*, John Rawls offered a new intellectual defense of the liberal concept of social well-being. Rejecting the linkage made by utilitarianism between the good (the satisfaction of individual desires) and the right (that which maximizes the good across individuals), Rawls argued that justice should be viewed as a problem of rational choice regarding the principles that will govern the basic structure of society. The first problem facing a theory of justice for Rawls, solved by his now famous "original position," was to conceptualize a fair procedure by which everyone would select the same principles of justice. The second was to explain what principles would actually be chosen from the original position.

According to Rawls, there were two principles that ultimately would be selected as principles of justice from the original position. While his most recent formulation of them has changed somewhat, the core ideas remain the same. As stated in his most recent book, *Political Liberalism*, the principles are that

> "a. Each person has an equal claim to a fully adequate scheme of equal basic rights and liberties, which scheme is compatible with the same scheme for all; and in this scheme the equal

political liberties, and only those liberties, are to be guaranteed their fair value.

"b. Social and economic inequalities are to satisfy two conditions: first, they are to be attached to positions and offices open to all under conditions of fair equality of opportunity; and second, they are to be of the greatest benefit to the least advantaged members of society." (Columbia University Press, 1993, pp. 5-6.)

Serially ordered, these two principles are to regulate the basic political, economic, and social institutions found in society.

Much has been written about Rawls' theory of justice in general and his principles of justice in particular. Given our interest in the modern liberal concept of social well-being, there are a number of things worth noting about each. First, Rawls saw himself explicitly articulating in philosophical terms the liberal values regarding social well-being which had come to dominate America's pluralistic political culture. His theory of justice was "a guiding framework designed to focus our moral sensibilities and to put before our intuitive capacities more limited and manageable questions for judgment." (*A Theory of Justice*, p. 53.) It explained how twentieth-century liberal concerns over social and economic inequality could be (and in fact were) balanced against more fundamental concerns over political liberty, and why the state had to intrude into the economy in order to guarantee social justice.

Second, Rawls offered liberals a way to sort out the sticky problem of the relationship between individual well-being and social well-being. As noted above, lurking in the background of the utilitarian defense of liberal values was the uncomfortable possibility that the welfare of a single person might be legitimately sacrificed on the altar of society's larger well-being. Rawls finessed the problem first by rejecting the idea that social justice must be linked to any particular idea of the good life or any particular notion of what constitutes human happiness. In the original position, people exist behind a veil of ignorance, not knowing who they are or what sort of life plan they will value. The principles of justice chosen in the original position thus are not concerned with the good life *per se* but with the "primary goods" in life, those goods that are needed to pursue any rational plan in life. Primary goods included such things as basic political rights and liberties, institutional opportunities and prerogatives of office and position, and income and wealth. (See *A Theory of Justice*, pp. 90-94; and *Political Liberalism*, pp. 178-190.) A just society was one that assured citizens that they would be provided with a fair share of the primary goods needed to pursue their own particular life plans.

Rawls' theory of justice also provided a sophisticated way for thinking about society and the proper role of government. Society, Rawls argued, was best viewed as a cooperative venture for mutual advantage that is marked by a conflict as well as an identity of interests. The identity lies in the fact that cooperation makes possible a better life for all, not only in terms of protected liberty but in terms of material well-being. The conflict lies in how the fruits of social cooperation are to be divided among the citizenry. The Principles of Justice provide a way of assigning rights and duties to the basic institutions of society and of defining the proper distribution of the benefits and burdens of social cooperation. (*A Theory of Justice*, p. 4.) In turn, the purpose of government is to enact just legislation, that is, engage in activities that preserve certain political, social, and economic conditions. In terms of the second principle of distributive justice, Rawls conceives of government as being charged with four tasks: guaranteeing a competitive pricing system, bringing about full employment, guaranteeing a social minimum, and preventing a concentration of economic power that might be considered detrimental to the "fair value of political liberty and fair equality of opportunity." (*Id.*, pp. 275-277.) For all intents and purposes, Rawls' theory catalogued in philosophical terms the powers already assumed by the state in the economy since the New Deal.

Finally, Rawls also helped to sort out the question of how liberals should think about the problem of economic inequality introduced by capitalist economic development. From Rawls' perspective, the question facing twentieth-century political capitalist democracies was not whether social and economic inequality was bad, but what sort of social and economic inequalities were just and, hence, permissible. Rawls' answer—that social and economic inequalities were just if they were of greatest benefit to the least advantaged in society—clearly supported the liberal belief that the state had an affirmative duty to protect those at the bottom of the social order. Generating enormous amounts of wealth was not enough to legitimize the social and economic institutions of a modern capitalist society. A powerful state was needed to assure that newly created economic prosperity would be fairly shared.

Rawls' theory of justice spawned an enormous literature over the next twenty years, not the least of which dealt directly with the problems of individual and social well-being. (See, for example, M. Sandel, *Liberalism and the Limits of Justice*, Cambridge University Press, 1982; J. Griffin, *Well-Being: Its Meaning, Measurement and Moral Importance*, Oxford University Press, 1986; A. Sen, *On Ethics and Economics*, B. Blackwell, 1987; A. Sen, *Inequality Reexamined*, cited above; A. Sen, "Capability and Well-Being," in M. Nussbaum and A. Sen, eds., *The Quality of Life*, Oxford University Press, 1993; W. Galston, *Liberal Purposes*, Cambridge University Press, 1991; and P. Dasgupta, *An Inquiry into Well-Being and Destitution*, Oxford University Press, 1993.) One of the most interesting and revealing responses is found in the work of Amartya Sen. According to Sen, Rawls' primary goods metric in the original position failed to satisfy the same needs in differently situated people. Human beings are diverse. Not all are able to transform the same bundle of primary goods into the same freedoms or the same well-being in their lives. Women convert primary goods into life opportunities differently than men, the disabled differently than those who are not, and the poor differently than the rich. Hence, a fully just society must address these concerns, not only those of Rawls' primary goods. Calling for a "capability-based" approach to well-being, Sen thus sought to turn attention away from the question of individual well-being, and away from that of equal commodities and resources, to that of those "functionings which are seen as constitutive elements of human well-being." (*Inequality Reexamined*, p. 190.)

Sen's arguments regarding social well-being and the state mirrored changes that were going on in the larger political culture throughout the 1980s and the 1990s. An increasing number of left-leaning politicians were expressing dissatisfaction with the view of social well-being that had dominated their political culture since the 1930s. Some argued that the state had to abandon the value neutrality proudly proclaimed by philosophers like Rawls and actively defend certain ways of life. (See Galston, 1991.) Others maintained that the state had a duty to intervene more actively in society and the economy to address long-festering problems centering around racial and gender inequity.

Sen's capabilities approach to the problem of justice directly reflected such political concerns. It demanded a much deeper inquiry than Rawls was willing to make into what constitutes a properly functioning human being or what constitutes the good life. Curiously, Sen himself appeared to be reluctant to make the kind of inquiry into the human good that might be necessary for his project to be completed. Indeed, he seemed to believe that the willingness to accept a plurality of answers to the question of the human good is a strength, not a weakness, to his theory. (See "Capability and Well-Being.") But whatever reluctance existed in Sen's mind regarding the nature of the good life or the exact composition of human well-being, there was none regarding the political imperative that follows from his work: a more activist and interventionist state that moved well beyond that envisioned by New Deal or Great Society liberals in the political world or by Rawls in *A Theory of Justice*. (But see *Political Liberalism*, pp. 183-187.)

Sen's criticism of Rawls' theory of justice is but one indication of the unraveling of the consensus on the left over the liberal concept of social well-being. Other criticisms can be found in the work of so-called civic liberals who have argued that we must rethink our fundamental notion of what community in America is all about. (See R. Bellah et al., *Habits of the Heart*, University of California Press, 1985, and *The Good Society*, Knopf, 1986; and W. Sullivan, *Reconstructing Public Philosophy*, University of California Press, 1988.) But the disagreements that divide mainstream liberals like Rawls from Sen and civic liberals pale in significance when contrasted to those raised by modern day conservatives. To the conservative concept of social well-being we now turn.

III

Historians remind us that what we call "conservatism" arose first as a European critique of the French Revolution and the rationalistic ideology upon which it fed. It soon became an overall criticism of modernity. The industrialization of the traditional economy, the concentration of power in the hands of the nation state, the secularization of human life, the rationalization of human thought, and the decline of traditional religious, moral, cultural and political values were all seen as conditions that brought disorder to society, making it difficult for individuals to live healthy, meaningful lives. To save society from the onslaught of modernity, conservatives argued, people had to be taught some important political lessons: There were limits to both reason and politics. Neither human beings nor human society was capable of perfection. Nevertheless, there was a moral order to the universe guaranteed by God. Building a good society meant maintaining the proper traditions, customs, and religious attitudes that would mold healthy and happy individuals.

In the 1950s, a small group of intellectuals tried to articulate a conservative perspective for American political life that could challenge the overwhelming liberal consensus that had followed from the New Deal. In the *Essays in the Public Philosophy* (New American Library, 1956), the popular journalist Walter Lippmann expressed concerns over America's materialistic civilization. He believed that a public philosophy grounded on the belief in an objective moral order was needed for constitutional government to work and was convinced that this was being undercut by the ever-present desire to have more material things. Two political philosophers who sympathized with Lippmann that there was a spiritual crisis in America were Leo Strauss and Eric Voegelin. For Strauss, the crisis of modernity lay in the rise of the idea of natural right and the corresponding decline in the idea of natural law. For Voegelin, the problem lay in the emergence of a gnostic world view, where man no longer admired the intrinsic order of the universe. Their calls for spiritual reform echoed the sentiments of traditional European conservative thought. (See N. O'Sullivan, *Conservatism*, St. Martin's Press, 1976, pp. 131-132.) But perhaps the most influential of these writers was Russell Kirk. Setting out to identify a viable tradition of Anglo-American conservative thought stretching back to the American Revolution, Kirk effectively sought to "Americanize" European conservatism.

These traditional conservative ideas held some appeal to American intellectuals concerned with the general problem of social well-being, but their appeal was limited. The antimodernism of this brand of European conservatism flew in the face of one important aspect of American political life—the ever-present desire for improved material well-being. America lacked the aristocratic traditions that were suspicious of capitalism and that became the seed bed of conservative politics in Europe. People came to America not so much to maintain the past as to build a more prosperous future. And there was the rub. How could a conservative approach to political life be made appealing to mainstream American thought?

The origins of what I refer to as the "modern conservative" view of social well-being do not lie in the work of any of these writers. Their fundamental inability to come to terms with twentieth-century capitalism left them on the outside looking in at a political and economic world they could criticize but in which they could never feel completely comfortable. The origins of a modern conservative perspective, in fact, lay in a very different place.

In 1944, the expatriate Austrian economist Friedrich Hayek published a book entitled *The Road to Serfdom*. Restating and updating the classical liberal ideas of David Hume and Adam Smith, Hayek launched a comprehensive attack on collectivist ideals. Fascism and communism weren't the only dangers facing free societies in the twentieth century; the expanding welfare state itself threatened to sap the nation of the liberty and institutions that were necessary for a modern society to prosper. Serialized in the *Reader's Digest*, *The Road to Serfdom* reached a wide popular audience in America. (See T. Rosenof, "Freedom, Planning and Totalitarianism: The Reception of F.A. Hayek's *Road to Serfdom*," *Canadian Review of American Studies*, Vol. 5, 1974; and A. Brinkley, "The Problem of American Conservatism," *American Historical Review*, Vol. 99, 1994.) Hayek himself renounced the mantle of "conservative." (See F.A. Hayek, *The Constitution of Liberty*, University of Chicago Press, 1960.) However, his ideas proved to be attractive to those Americans who, on the one hand, continued to believe in the material promise of American life but, on the other hand, were highly suspicious of the expanding power of the state.

Milton Friedman's popular book, *Capitalism and Freedom* (University of Chicago Press, 1962), built upon many of the ideas articulated in Hayek's work. A monetarist who helped revive the quantity theory of money, Friedman argued that economic freedom was an essential component of political freedom, and capitalism was a necessary prerequisite for a free political society. In the work of Friedman and other economists like James Buchanan and Gordon Tullock, a modern conservative way of looking at the problem of social well-being began to emerge. (See C. Waligorski, *The Political Theory of the*

Conservative Economists, University Press of Kansas, 1990.)

Unlike traditional conservatives who remained distrustful of the capitalist and materialistic life spawned by modernity, modern conservatives embraced it. Continued material prosperity was an essential dimension of social well-being for the modern conservative, and capitalism was perceived to be the most efficient social system yet discovered in history that could bring this about. The secret to capitalism's success lay in the way that it harnessed and coordinated the actions of innumerable individuals through the free market mechanism. The danger to material prosperity and general social well-being thus lay not in the capitalist economy, but in an expanding government that could destroy the motivational and institutional foundations of the free market economy.

The spin given on the origins of the Great Depression by modern conservatives like Milton Friedman reveals the wide gulf separating modern liberalism from modern conservatism. According to the new conservative historiography, the state did not save the capitalist economy from itself, as the liberal mythology held. To be sure, there was a bad recession in the late 1920s. But there had been bad recessions in the past from which the economy had naturally recovered. What made this one so bad was the action of the state itself. Through the misguided deflationary actions of the Federal Reserve System in the early 1930s, a serious economic recession was transformed into a devastating depression. Thus the state, not the capitalist economy, was the root of the problem.

Modern conservatism sharply departed from the modern liberal notion of social well-being on two issues—equity and private virtue. It rejected the idea that a positive duty of government in a democratic society was to eliminate the inequalities that emerged from economic development. Inequality was an inevitable part of any dynamic economy. As long as these inequalities were not being artificially maintained through government action, over the long run they would serve the general public good by encouraging individuals to act in socially beneficial ways.

The real problems came when the government tried to force the distribution of wealth permanently in one direction or another through social welfare programs. Such well-intentioned programs had numerous unintended consequences that were detrimental to social well-being in the long run. Friedman noted, for example, that such legislation sent out the wrong signals in the market place as to what economic activities were valuable and what were not. Price distortions would wreak economic havoc over the long run, create a serious misallocation of resources in the nation's economy, and undermine future economic growth. Worse yet, redistributive programs sponsored by the state could shut off other lines of institutional development that might have contributed even more to social well-being. As

Hayek noted in his 1960 book, *The Constitution of Liberty*, "If we commit ourselves to a single comprehensive organization because its immediate coverage is greater, we may well prevent the evolution of other organizations whose eventual contribution to welfare might have been greater." (P. 288.) In the modern world, provisions probably had to be made to maintain a certain level of subsistence for all citizens. However, for Hayek, the very idea of social justice was a dangerous illusion propagated by special interests seeking to use the state on their own behalf.

The second issue separating modern liberals from modern conservatives was that of private virtue. For all intents and purposes, liberals took the existence of moral capital in society as the starting point of their analysis. For the most part, they assumed that providing individuals with more income would make them, and hence society, better off. Not surprisingly, they were reluctant to make value judgments about the poor themselves.

For example, the War on Poverty's Community Action programs were predicated on the idea that the poor themselves were in the best position to understand what had to be done to address the poverty problem. Poverty was an income problem, not a moral problem. The state's job was to help the poor help themselves. Similar assumptions are found in Rawls' theory of Justice as Fairness. For Rawls, questions of justice were logically distinct from questions of the good life. The principles of justice assumed that individuals followed some rational life plan. This postulate meant that the state could safely remain neutral on the question of the good life. But what if individuals didn't pursue a rational life plan? What if individuals adopted a pathological style of life that had terrible consequences for themselves and society as a whole? How could the War on Poverty work or Rawls' principles of justice be applied in such circumstances?

Such problems provided a starting point for the modern conservative perspective on private virtue. Moral capital in society could not be taken as a given. It had to be rebuilt in every generation. But how? The modern conservative answer to this question differed sharply from that offered by both modern liberals and traditional conservatives. Like other forms of capital, moral capital came out of the workings of a free market economy and the social and political institutions underlying it. Historically, the market had freed individuals from the chains of social hierarchy found in traditional societies. By enabling individuals to take control of their own lives, the market also molded the moral character of the people by rewarding certain forms of behavior and punishing others. By creating morally responsible individuals, it guaranteed that individual well-being and social well-being would come together.

From the modern conservative perspective, state intervention in the economy threatened general social well-being in two ways. First, by distorting the signals provided by market prices, it severed the linkage that tied individual self-interest to the general public good in the long run. Second, state intervention, particularly those actions in pursuit of equity, destroyed the moral capital upon which the nation's future prosperity was built.

What followed from this understanding of state intervention was a view of twentieth-century American history that stood in sharp relief to the liberal Whiggish view discussed earlier. Far from being the culminating glory of American history, the growth of the state represented the intensifying corruption found throughout all American society in the twentieth century. New regulatory programs were not indicative of a growing public sector that curtailed and redirected private interest for the public good. On the contrary, they were proof positive that the public sector at last had been conquered by private interests. Similarly, new welfare programs did not reflect a society honestly coming to grips with its problems, but the ongoing breakdown of the nation's moral capital.

The popularity of the modern conservative historical view of the state undoubtedly lay partly in the fact that it echoed the republican and civic humanist values that have been identified with national political life since the founding. (See J. Pocock, *The Machiavellian Moment*, Princeton University Press, 1975; and F. McDonald, *Novus Ordo Seclorum: The Intellectual Origins of the Constitution*, University Press of Kansas, 1985.) Since the time of the Roman Republic, republican writers have long bemoaned the betrayal of the public good by self-interested political actors. Decrying the corruption found in the public world, they called upon individuals to transcend their narrow selfish interests for the larger public good.

The modern conservative version of republicanism put a fascinating new twist on traditional republican themes. Economic self-interest could be directed to serve the larger public good as long as it did not spill over into political affairs. On its own, capitalist economic activity could be expected to create the material and moral conditions needed for a society to prosper. But once economic self-interest intruded into politics and legislative action, all bets were off, and the question of social well-being was up for grabs.

The modern conservative concept of social well-being grew in popularity throughout the 1960s and 1970s. The newly founded Public Choice School of Economics served as a vehicle for the exploration of conservative themes. A Neoconservative Movement sympathetic to modern conservatism emerged out a group of intellectuals who felt that American liberalism had gone astray in the years following the Great Society. (See G. Dorrien, *The Neoconservative Mind*, Temple University Press, 1993.) Think tanks and foundations amenable to conservative ideas emerged to support young conservative scholars. (See P. Gottfried, *The Conservative Movement*, Twayne Publishers, 1992.) For the most part during this period, however, the modern conservative concept of social well-being was dwarfed by triumphant liberalism. And then came the sea change.

Much like the period following World War I, the late 1970s and early 1980s were a time of economic turmoil characterized by stagflation. Following the 1974-75 recession, the change in the rate of inflation accelerated increasing from 6.3 percent in 1976, to 8.8 percent in 1979, and peaking at 9.6 percent in 1982. While change in the rate of growth in real GDP per capita picked up in the early years of the Carter administration, it collapsed in 1979, bottoming out finally in 1982. Meanwhile, unemployment rose from 4.8 percent in 1973, to 8.3 percent in 1975, and peaking in 1982 and 1983 at 9.5 percent. Although the standard of living for the average American had increased steadily since the end of World War II, that rise came to an abrupt halt in 1973, and the standard of living declined throughout the remainder of the decade. (See Berry, Harpham, and Elliott, 1995.)

Intensifying stagflation brought on a general feeling of economic malaise throughout the nation. Gone was the liberal certainty that the government could micromanage the economy back to prosperity again. By the end of the Carter administration, Democrats and Republicans alike spoke of the end of the New Deal coalition and the brand of liberalism that it had brought to American political life.

The election of Ronald Reagan signaled the full arrival of the conservative concept of social well-being on the national scene. The Reagan message of getting the government off the backs of the people through lower taxes, deregulation, and welfare cuts touched a chord in the American psyche. While this conservative orientation would not replace liberal views in the policy arena, it successfully challenged the liberal hegemony which had reigned since the New Deal. Nowhere was this challenge more apparent than in the debates over social security and welfare reform that took place throughout the 1980s.

The economic troubles of the 1970s placed a dagger at the heart of the social security pension system and the liberal consensus that it represented. The 1972 reforms which indexed old age pensions to the cost of living were suppose to have depoliticized the program by guaranteeing the real value of benefits and ensuring adequate funding. Instead, accelerating inflation and chronically high unemployment provided a recipe for disaster as benefit payouts began to lag behind tax contributions. Short-term financial difficulties were only part of the problem. Long-term demographic changes, conveniently ignored while the indexing proposals were being put into place, painted a grim picture of the future of the nation's largest income maintenance program. Social security was becoming a mature social insurance program. The ratio of workers contributing to the program to beneficiaries was declining, and the tax burden per worker was increasing. Moreover, the baby boom generation was being followed by a baby bust. However unfavorable the worker to beneficiary ratio was in the 1970s, it was only going to get worse in the second and third decades of the twenty-first century. By the end of the Carter years, it was difficult to see how the pay-as-you-go formula could continue to work as a builder of the liberal consensus. By the end of the Reagan years, it was clear that it couldn't.

The solutions to the financial troubles plaguing social security adopted by Congress during the late 1970s and early 1980s were controversial and not particularly innovative. Payroll taxes were raised, and the burden shifted upward to those with higher incomes. Between 1979 and 1992, the overall payroll tax rose from 6.13 percent on a wage base of $22,900 to 7.65 percent on $55,500, a sum matched by the worker's employer. The maximum amount that could be deducted from an employee's payroll check thus rose from $1,404 per year to $4,246, a 300 percent increase. Selected benefits were cut for the first time in the history of the program and the retirement age was raised over a period of years from sixty-five to sixty-seven. Finally, provisions were made for the accumulation of a trust fund that would help pay for the benefits that baby boomers were promised to receive in the twenty-first century. It was calculated that the reforms would keep the system solvent until around 2025, at which time retirement of the baby boom generation would overwhelm it.

These financial controversies gave credibility to the modern conservative criticism of the expanding welfare state. It was difficult to sell the social security program as a rationally planned social insurance program that would benefit everyone at some point in time. For an increasing number of scholars, politicians, and young workers, the pay-as-you-go system was seen to be a government sponsored Ponzi scheme where those who were in first benefitted the most, and those in last benefitted the least. The idea that the social security system represented a fair social contract across generations maintained by the state was also subject to question. The very notion that one generation could commit a generation yet unborn to programs that might or might not serve their own generational well-being became suspect. (A. H. Robertson, *The Coming Revolution in Social Security*, Reston Pub. Co., 1981; C. Weaver, *The Crisis of Social Security: Economic and Political Origins*, Duke University Press, 1982; and P. Laslett and J. Fishkin, eds., *Justice Between Age Groups and Generations*, Yale University Press, 1992.)

The bitter and vitriolic politics surrounding the reform debate made it increasingly difficult to maintain the liberal myth that social security impartially served the interests of everyone in society. But in certain respects, the myth was no longer needed. Interest group politics had come to replace liberal consensus as the defining feature of the politics of social security reform in the 1980s. By the end of Reagan's first term in office, it became increasingly clear that the elderly were one of the most powerful lobbies in Washington. For all intents and purposes, they held an effective veto power over any initiatives brought forward that might hurt their interests. Everyone became afraid to touch "the third rail" of American politics, social security. Following the electoral debacle of 1982, which was brought on in large part by Reagan's call to reform social security at the margins, even Republicans came to preach the inviolability of the social security compact with the elderly.

By the 1990s, the worst fears of modern conservatives regarding the politics of social security reform had been realized. The program had become a straitjacket from which the nation could not escape. Alternative pension arrangements that might have proved attractive to younger members of the population were effectively kept off the national agenda by powerful lobbying efforts. While the short-run financial problems facing the social security system were put to bed, the long-run question of the baby boom generation loomed in the not too distant future. The liberal dream of an expanding state providing material prosperity to the nation's elderly had been replaced by the conservative nightmare of a coming national reckoning.

A second area where the modern conservative concept of social well-being affected public discourse in the 1980s was in the debate over welfare reform. The Great Society ended with a general disillusionment over the liberal approach to welfare reform. Simply getting money to the poor so that they could help themselves did not seem to work. Soaring welfare rolls and escalating costs throughout the late 1960s and early 1970s led many to conclude that there was something fundamentally wrong with welfare policy as it had been practiced since the New Deal. As welfare rolls leveled off in the mid-1970s, concern began to shift to a new set of issues centering around the question of welfare dependency and moral character. Why had the War on Poverty not worked? Was it simply a question of inadequate funding and weak political will, or were more fundamental moral issues at stake? Had well-intentioned liberal policies in the past backfired, harming the very individuals liberals were seeking to assist? By making people directly dependent upon the state for their economic well-being, had the state undermined certain individuals' ability to take care of themselves? (See L. Mead, *The New Politics of Poverty*, Basic Books, 1992.)

Two books that played a major role in defining the new politics of dependency were George Gilder's *Wealth and Poverty* (Bantam Books, 1981) and Charles Murray's *Losing Ground* (Basic Books, 1984). Gilder preached a modern conservative gospel of faith in the market, hard work, and family values that was suspicious of all governmental attempts to make people better off. Like many other conservatives in the early Reagan administration, Gilder believed that the welfare state was destroying the cultural capital that enabled individuals to escape poverty and facilitated the production of increased national wealth. Charles Murray took this argument one step further. Through a detailed empirical analysis, Murray tried to show why the social policies of the Great Society years were misguided. By providing welfare to more people and removing many of the social taboos surrounding it, well intentioned policy had actively encouraged people to behave in a way that was socially dysfunctional. Welfare may have made people better off monetarily, but it robbed them of something that was much more important to their personal well-being—the character traits and moral values that would enable them to escape their current condition. Murray's solution to the problem of welfare dependency was harsh: Eliminate all welfare programs that destroyed an individual's willingness to work. Let the market reinstill among the poor the values of hard work and discipline that had enabled earlier generations of poor people to improve their lot in life.

The empirical findings of *Losing Ground* were subject to scathing criticism in the years immediately following its publication. Liberal academics, in particular, were quick to reject many of the quantitative arguments developed by Murray. Critics assailed Murray's methods as faulty, his arguments as misconstrued, and his conclusions and proposals as insupportable. But all too often, these criticisms missed what was really at stake in Murray's book. *Losing Ground* was not meant to be the definitive quantitative study of the poverty problem. It was a political tract which sought to redefine the way policy makers thought about the general problem of poverty in the late twentieth century. (See E. Harpham and R. Scotch, "Rethinking the War on Poverty," *Western Political Quarterly*, March 1988.) Along with Murray's later book, *In Pursuit of Happiness and Good Government* (Simon and Schuster, 1988), it articulated powerfully the modern conservative vision of the linkage that joined individual well-being to social well-being.

As a political tract, *Losing Ground* was enormously successful. Its themes about dependency and the creation of an underclass by misguided public policy would resonate even through the work of strident defenders of liberal values in the late 1980s. (See W. Wilson, *The Truly Disadvantaged: The Inner City, the Underclass, and Public Policy*, University of Chicago Press, 1987; and D. Ellwood, *Poor Support*, Basic Books, 1988.) But its full impact can best be seen in the new consensus that was developing in the late 1980s and early 1990s over welfare policy. Policy makers and the public recognized a problem of welfare dependency in America: An underclass of socially dysfunctional individuals had been created and sustained by existing governmental policy. The question was what should be done?

By the fall of 1994, the answer appeared to be one heavily influenced by the modern conservative perspective—increased work requirements, improved support programs that would encourage and enable people to work, and benefit termination for those who continued to pursue a recalcitrant life style. Through a reformed welfare system, the state would attempt to accomplish the most conservative of political goals—instilling private virtue in the hearts of those members of society who were no longer part of the mainstream.

The rediscovery of this politics of virtue extended far beyond the welfare debates of the 1980s and early 1990s, bringing traditional conservative and modern conservative ideas about social well-being closer together. (See B. Frohnen, *Virtue and the Promise of Conservatism*, University of Press of Kansas, 1993.) In *Statecraft as Soulcraft*, the popular conservative commentator George Will called upon Americans to recognize an undeniable truth: Government was in the business of moral education. According to Will, "We need a public philosophy that can rectify the current imbalance between the political order's meticulous concern for material well-being and its fastidious withdrawal from concern for the inner lives and moral character of citizens." (Simon and Schuster, 1983: p. 65.) Similar sentiments echo throughout William F. Buckley, Jr.'s *Gratitude: Reflections on What We Owe our Country* (Random House, 1990). Americans, Buckley argued, had lost a sense of the debts they owed to their homeland. He called upon government to establish a form of national service that could balance the materialistic drives in American culture with a new sense of republican citizenship.

Perhaps the clearest statements of the conservative politics of virtue can be found in a book of moral tales edited by William Bennett, the former Secretary of Education and Chairman of the National Endowment for the Humanities under Reagan. (*The Book of Virtues*, Simon and Schuster, 1993.) The book was intended to be used in the moral education of the young. Like other conservatives, Bennett did not believe that the nation's moral or cultural capital could be taken as a given. It had to be recreated and nourished in every generation. Instilling virtue in the hearts and minds of the young was one of the most important duties of the older generation. The book's popularity spoke to the fact that many Americans agreed with him. For American conservatives of all stripes, the general problem of social well-being was seen to be inextricably tied to the moral character of every individual in society.

IV

The 1994 off-year election invites us to ask whether liberal or conservative ideas provide the better way for thinking about American political life in the late 1990s. Choosing one perspective rather than the other will have important implications not only for how we view today but how we build tomorrow.

A good place to begin answering this question is by broadening our understanding of where we have been recently. Looking back on the 1980s, it is clear that more changed than just our political conceptions of social well-being. The American economy also went through a period of profound transformation. Between 1981 and 1988, the rate of inflation declined from 9.6 percent to 2.5 percent. In 1986, there was actual deflation in producer prices for the first time since 1949. During the expansion, the economy grew by 32 percent, employment rose by 19.5 percent, real per capita income increased by 18.8 percent, real manufacturing input rose by 48.3 percent, and the real value of U.S. exports grew by 92.6 percent. These macroeconomic figures, however, do not capture the full meaning of the economic changes of the 1980s. (See Berry, Harpham, and Elliott, 1995.)

Much like the 1920s, the 1980s were a period of capitalist creative destruction, when the forces of one technological regime were being rapidly replaced by another. Old industries and whole regional economies geared to assembly-line production went into decline. Companies such as AT&T and General Motors, long seen as centerpieces of American economic power, struggled to restructure or downsize themselves to meet the competitive demands of increasing international competition. Meanwhile, whole new industries based on advanced technologies sprang up to redefine the nation's economic landscape and to be the source of future economic growth.

One of the consequences of the technological transformation of the 1980s was the return of inequality as a pressing political issue. For the first time since the New Deal, the share of wealth and income of the wealthiest members of American society had risen, and the share of the poor had declined. Initially, a few political commentators argued that this inequality was primarily due to the regressive Reagan era tax cuts. (See B. Harrison and B. Bluestone, *The Great U-turn: Corporate Restructuring and the Polarizing of America*, Basic Books, 1988; and K. Phillips, *The Politics of the Rich and the Poor*, 1991, and *Boiling Point: Democrats, Republicans, and the Decline of Middle-Class Prosperity*, Random House, 1993.) But a consensus has recently emerged among many scholars that tax cuts were only part of the story. Most of the new inequality in the 1980s was probably due to changes in the labor markets brought on by economic restructuring. (See Berry, Harpham, and Elliott, 1995.)

The relevant political question for us today is what, if anything, should the government do to address the equity question? What institutions should be built, and which public policies should be implemented over the next twenty years to improve social well-being in the nation? Should we follow the example of the New Deal and Great Society by expanding the administrative capacity of the state, or should we follow a different path based on a different vision of the good society?

I would argue the latter. Campaign rhetoric aside, the 1990s are not the 1930s. We have not experienced an economic catastrophe along the lines of the Great Depression. Our basic economic and political institutions are intact and retain the support of the people. Few individuals advocate the overhaul of our capitalist institutions or the establishment of a socialized economy. Indeed, if there is one lesson that has come out of the 1980s, it is that highly centralized, overly bureaucratized societies are unable to cope with change over the long haul. Far from realizing the egalitarian dream of socialism, twentieth-century communist societies institutionalized a brand of bureaucratic conservatism at odds with everyone's well-being but those in power.

Our problem in America today is how to build institutions and implement public policies that are flexible enough to grapple with the economic and technical realities of life in the twenty-first century. In health care, for example, we face the question of reform (or at least we did for most of the summer). How should we go about reorganizing our complex system of private and public health care delivery? Should we build a New Deal style national health care system that guarantees "equal access" to all Americans? Or should we be more modest in our objectives, seeking to reform and redirect the forces of the market, rather than replacing them?

I believe that it is a serious mistake to try to build a New Deal-style national health care system. The idea that equal health care is a right is a noble one, but misses two important points. First, a centrally controlled, rigidly administered system of health care could kill the goose that lays the golden eggs. Science and technology are on the verge of major breakthroughs in the treatment of many chronic diseases that will change the way we think about health care. Properly encouraged, these breakthroughs could quickly ratchet up both individual and social well-being. Improperly encouraged, science and technology could be misdirected or shut down, and that would be a shame.

For generations, polio was a devastating disease. Through the 1950s, basic treatment comprised wheel chairs and iron lungs. Then came Jonas Salk's research and his vaccine. Polio became a preventable disease, and our world was changed for the better forever. One study recently estimated that the cost of polio treatment today would be $30 billion a year if there had been no Salk vaccine. (M. Kirschner, E. Marincola, and E.O. Teisberg, "The Role of Biomedical Research in Health Care Reform," *Science*, October 7, 1994.) This is an astounding figure, but one made even more disturbing when we note that the Clinton health care proposals made no mention of money for research. It is as if research and scientific breakthroughs were a gift from heaven that we could expect regardless of what we do to our institutions and policies.

But misdirecting or shutting down technological advancement in medicine is only part of the problem. Poorly designed micro-managed health care reforms could have other unintended effects that are, in many ways, more insidious and dangerous to social well-being. By having government assume direct control over the delivery and pricing of health care, we run the danger of making society, not the individual, responsible for his or her own well-being. The claim that equal health care is a right can easily deteriorate into the demand that it become a free good and that individuals not have to bear any of the costs or assume the responsibility for taking care of themselves. There are too many people around today who are willing to spend $20,000 for a new car but who gripe over paying a few extra dollars to take care of their own bodies. Is that the kind of responsible individual we want our health care system to spawn?

There is a role for government in medicine. Government should help people cope with personal medical catastrophes that are beyond their financial means. It should encourage them to take care of and invest in their bodies as they might any other piece of valuable property. It should teach them that there are costs associated with good health care, and that individuals should expect to have to pay for quality health care. A society, like an individual, gets what it pays for. A guaranteed $10 annual physical examination for your child may sound good in theory. But in practice it will soon become an annual exam not worth having.

My defense of modern conservatism must not be construed as an apology for anything that calls itself conservative. There are problems that haunt conservatism just as there are problems that haunt modern liberalism. A healthy distrust of state expansion can easily deteriorate into a reluctance to do anything in the political arena. A concern over promoting virtuous behavior can easily degenerate into a useless xenophobic moralism.

Recognizing that modern conservatism has its own tensions and problems should not blind us to the great lesson with which it leaves us: The capitalist economic system remains the most powerful lever for material progress yet developed in the history of the world. Our problem in the late twentieth century is not to build up a highly bureaucratized set of political institutions that will replace this system. We must, instead, build flexible ones that will complement it. I am not advocating pure laissez faire. There is a proper role for government and politics in directing the economic life of the nation. But this role differs sharply from that envisioned by modern liberals since the New Deal. Discovering exactly what the optimal limits and extent of government should be in a dynamic high tech economy may be the greatest political challenge we face over the next few decades. In the end, I believe that we will learn that the proper role of government is not to protect people from the market. It is to teach and encourage them to be independent and responsible citizens, free individuals who are able use the market for their own and society's well-being.

In closing, I would like to remember the words of Lord Acton, a famous nineteenth-century classical liberal. At the end of his Inaugural Lecture as the Regis Professor of History at Cambridge, he bid his students to "look with remorse upon the past, and to the future with assured hope of better things." Republicans assuming power in both houses of congress for the first time in over forty years would do well to look at the world with the vision of Lord Acton. So would we.

AMBIGUITIES AND IRONIES: LIBERALISM AND CONSERVATISM IN THE AMERICAN TRADITION

by

Wilson Carey McWilliams

Wilson Carey McWilliams

Wilson Carey McWilliams is Professor of Political Science at Rutgers University, New Brunswick, New Jersey, where he has taught since 1970. He received his A.B., M.A., and Ph.D. from the University of California (Berkeley) and, before coming to Rutgers, he taught at Oberlin College and Brooklyn College. He has also served as a visiting professor at Yale and at Haverford College.

McWilliams has directed nine summer seminars for teachers for the National Endowment for the Humanities and two institutes for the New Jersey Council for the Humanities. In 1989, he was awarded the John Witherspoon Award for Distinguished Service to the Humanities. He has served as Vice President (1991-1992) and Secretary (1974-1975) of the American Political Science Association, and since the founding of the institute, he has been Vice President of the Institute for the Study of Civil Values.

He writes chiefly on American politics and political thought, with a special emphasis on the relation between politics and religion. His books include The Idea of Fraternity in America *(1973), which won the National Historical Society Prize, and he has co-authored studies of the elections of 1976, 1980, 1984, 1988 and 1992. In addition to scholarly articles, he contributes frequently to* Commonweal *and other journals of opinion. He is currently working on a study of the political thought of Mark Twain.*

Active in civic and community affairs, Professor McWilliams is an Elder of the Flemington Presbyterian Church, a Trustee of the Hunterdon County Historical Society, and Chair of the Municipal Democratic Committee of Flemington, New Jersey.

AMBIGUITIES AND IRONIES: CONSERVATISM AND LIBERALISM IN THE AMERICAN POLITICAL TRADITION

by

Wilson Carey McWilliams

Back in 1963, when my father spoke at the University of Oregon, the local reporter had a hard time squaring the man with the liberal paragon. For one thing, he didn't look the part; among other things, he parted his hair straight down the middle (a habit he had learned, although the reporter didn't know it, from H. L. Mencken). And as the reporter told it, while he ended his speech sounding like John Kenneth Galbraith, he "took off like Billy Graham" with an indictment of public morals—including the quiz show scandals, recently brought back into memory—that had the accents of an evangelical revival. (*Eugene Register-Guard*, October 23, 1963, p. B1.) In fact, a few months earlier, when my father participated in a forum with Russell Kirk, the conservative publicist, the *Minnesota Daily* headline ran, "Kirk, McWilliams Call for Return to Traditional Ethic." (February 19, 1963, p. 1.)

Not that such conflicting images are unusual in American politics. In this century, the most liberal Protestant denominations, the Friends and the Unitarians, have been represented in the White House by Hoover, Nixon, and William Howard Taft; the three Baptists to hold the presidency—Truman, Carter, and Clinton—have been at least a little to the left of center. Ronald Reagan was a hero for conservatives, and religious conservatives in particular, even though he had been divorced, rarely attended church, and had a habit of quoting Tom Paine, that old infidel. Reagan even had a special fondness for Paine's dictum that "We have it in our power to begin the world over again," a proclamation of human mastery that, Paine goes on to say, holds out the possibility of undoing the pattern of history since Noah, a vision that implies overcoming the alienation of humanity from nature, if not original sin itself. (*The Complete Writings of Thomas Paine*, Vol. I, ed. Philip S. Foner, Citadel, 1969, 45.) Go figure: In American usage, the terms "liberal" and "conservative" are profoundly ambiguous, including elements that are often inconsistent and never without a proportion of irony.

In the first place, we preserve the original and enduring meaning in which liberal and conservative refer, not to ideologies and parties, but to temperaments, dispositions of the soul. (Even at the outset, I need to introduce a caveat and an ambiguity. Nobody is all one thing or the other; every soul has its liberalities and its Tory corners. Still, the distinction helps in identifying patterns and dominant principles.) Understood in relation to character, a conservative is someone inclined to cherish what has been received, and to transmit an inheritance, not strictly unaltered, but in a way that preserves continuity, a link with the past and with origins. Conservatives value rituals, the old ways of doing and remembering, and they hold up examples from the past as models for aspiration, footsteps on a path to excellence that is both tried and distinctively one's own.

A conservative, Ambrose Bierce wrote, is "enamored of existing evils, as distinguished from the liberal, who wishes to replace them with others." (*The Devil's Dictionary*, World, 1941, pp. 54-55.) Just so: In the conservative view, change is suspect, and while conservatives acknowledge its inevitability, they do so without enthusiasm or moral celebration. The hope of reform, conservatives know, often results in something worse; meddling can damage parts of a regime that prove to be unsuspectedly fundamental. Order is precious and at least a little fragile. Conservatives treat it delicately, observing the forms; at least outwardly, they accept the limits of convention and respect established authority. And they regard it as the task of moral education to shape individuals to fit the existing order of things, developing those virtues and attitudes that suit the regime and its laws.

Liberals, by contrast, are defined by liberality. They are more inclined to give than to save, and since growth permits generosity without loss, liberals are temperamentally prone to look for the possibility of improvement. When liberals speak of continuity or traditions, they are likely to be thinking of ways in which an inheritance can be amplified or perfected; their vision is generally promethean rather than epimethean. Even in a relatively good society, liberals are apt to embrace change, trusting in their ability to separate what is essential from what is accidental or excrescent, crafting new skins for the wine of new times.

The liberal imagination depreciates forms in favor of substance and is likely to be attracted to theory at the expense of practice, asking us, as John Rawls does, to step behind a "veil of ignorance" that, by obscuring the lessons of experience, is thought to clarify first principles. (*A Theory of Justice*, Harvard University Press, 1971, pp. 12, 19, 136-142.) As that suggests, liberals habitually question and challenge authority, holding convention to the standard of the unconventional—to nature, or more recently, the creative will—so that "conventional," in liberal rhetoric, connotes contempt. A regime, in the liberal view, should adapt itself to the needs and wants of individuals, who are the measure of politics and perhaps of all things, as in Protagoras' ancient humanistic affirmation.

Similarly, liberals incline to see most communities and social relationships in terms of their utility to the individuals they comprise, and hence properly redefined or abandoned in response to changes in one's stage of life or historical developments. Individuals should be freed from the constraint of particular bonds to move toward relationships that are more inclusive, liberals hold, even though such broader relationships may sacrifice depth and intensity. A conservative, on the other hand, will be more concerned to preserve existing communities and bonds that are particular, historic, and hence relatively exclusive. In Marxist terms, in any choice between the dynamic "modes of production" and the "social relationships of production" which "fetter" them, a conservative will pick the social relationships every time; a liberal will be more willing to identify the modes of production with progress and freedom. (Karl Marx and Friedrich Engels, *The Communist Manifesto*, trans. Samuel Moore, Penguin, 1967, pp. 82, 86.) Liberals, in other words, look to make new friends, conservatives to keep old ones.

Finally, each temperament has its distinctive vices or excesses. Liberals are tempted to be profligate, squandering inherited cultural resources as well as money. Their ostensible warmth is often superficial, without intimacy or willingness to sacrifice, loving humankind but neglecting their own. Conservatives, by contrast, can be narrow and mean-spirited, hoarding in a way that loses sight of the future, clinging to outworn forms, sometimes gracefully, but indifferent to human pain. If the liberal nightmare is Mrs. Jellyby in *Bleak House*, conservatives are haunted by *A Tale of Two Cities* and the Marquis St. Evremonde.

But personality is not the whole story. Conservative and liberal also refer to more or less coherent ideologies that took shape from the late seventeenth century through the age of the democratic revolution, down to sometime around 1848. A sketch of those doctrines seems in order.

Rooted in the teachings of Hobbes and Locke, and given a new, idealized form by Kant, liberalism begins by approaching politics in a secular spirit, holding that religion is properly governed if not defined by social and political utility. Liberty is liberalism's lodestar: Individuals are endowed with rights or moral autonomy. Nature, at most the source of rights, poses obstacles but no moral limits to human striving; human beings are naturally engaged in a struggle to master nature. Society possibly and government certainly are humanly contrived and constructed, designed to protect rights and satisfy desires, so that ideally, government—lacking independent moral authority—is reduced to a matter of administration and technique.

Since human beings, in liberal theory, properly begin with equal rights and opportunities, inequalities are justified only as the prize of individual achievements, especially in the war against nature. Class conveys no moral title. Liberalism is at least suspicious of inheritance (although inclined to concede its utility) or of any claim based on birth; liberal teaching, consequently, strains against inequalities of race and gender, even when liberals accept them in practice. The free market—in goods but also in ideas—emerged as liberalism's ark of the social covenant. Commerce commended itself to liberal theorists for its ability to undermine boundaries, weakening custom subtly and ordinarily without violence. In the age of the bourgeoisie, Marx and Engels wrote of the market, "National one-sidedness and narrow-mindedness become more and more impossible. . . . [T]he cheap prices of its commodities are the heavy artillery with which it batters down all Chinese walls." Like liberalism itself, the market works to erode the idea of natural qualities or ranks. "All fixed, fast-frozen relations . . . are swept away," Marx and Engels observed; "all new ones become antiquated before they can ossify," a tendency liberal doctrinaires equated with progress and with freedom. (*The Communist Manifesto*, pp. 83-84.) To sum up, historic liberal ideology rests on three pillars—secularism, individualism, and free exchange—simplified still further by the nineteenth-century battle cry, "Free markets and free men."

Conservatism is a somewhat more complicated matter because, in its origins, it combined those who upheld the Old Regime from principle and those, like Burke, who did so chiefly for reasons of prudence. Still, conservative doctrine has its characteristic tenets and commonalities. (I am influenced, in what follows, by Russell Kirk's "six canons of conservatism" in *The Conservative Mind*, Gateway, 1954, pp. 7-8.) To begin with, conservatism admires reverence and is often disposed to regard religion as a shaping authority in secular life, one that defines what is truly human and truly useful, an inclination at least sympathetic to a religious establishment. (*The Works of Edmund Burke*, Vol. III, Little Brown, 1854, pp. 352-354.) Nature assigns human beings a place in the order of things, accompanied by laws and duties, and nature's teaching speaks less of natural rights than of what is naturally right. Conservative theorizing tends to view human beings as social, and sometimes as political, animals, and it is certain to affirm that political society is necessary to any fully human nature. As a moral being the individual is a product of society, or culture, or history; the terms vary with the theorist, but all conservatism sees humans as *situated* animals, decisively shaped if not defined by context. Necessary to human nurture, family and civil society have autonomous roles, but the "little platoon" is part of a larger regiment; the state has a magisterial mission and superintending authority. (*Works of Edmund Burke*, Vol. III, p. 392.)

Rank, the distinction of what is excellent from what is base, is inherent in moral ordering, and conservative teaching—respecting birth and tradition—regards the established classes as having at least "presumptive" virtue. (Harvey C. Mansfield, Jr., *Statesmanship and Party Government*, University of Chicago Press, 1965, pp. 201-223.) That doctrine, it should be obvious, admits a defense of inequalities based on race or gender, although the great conservative ideologues were chiefly concerned to support the hierarchies and continuities of social class. Conservatism suspected or despised the age of "sophists, economists and calculators," the market's tendency to displace quality in favor of quantity, with the pursuit of honor yielding to the quest for economic gain. (*Works of Edmund Burke*, Vol. III, p. 331.) For the sake of parallelism, conservative ideology can be reduced to three principles—religion, community, and ordered stability—that help to highlight its conflict with its liberal rival.

Obviously, there is an affinity between a liberal or conservative temperament and its corresponding doctrine, enough so that the two have often seemed all but equivalent. Early in the age of ideology, for example, Jefferson wrote Lafayette that the parties rested on a natural distinction between "healthy, strong and bold" Whigs, who cherished the people, and "sickly, weakly, timid" men, who, fearing the people, were Tories "by nature." (Letter to Lafayette, November 4, 1823, in *Life and Selected Writings of Thomas Jefferson*, ed. Adrienne Koch and William Peden, Modern Library, 1944, p. 712.) It ought to be clear, however, that the two things are not *identical*; by referring to some men as Tories by nature, Jefferson indicated that there were also Tories (or Whigs) by convention. In any given situation, what a conservative person hopes to preserve may or may not accord with conservative doctrine. In the last years of the Soviet Union, for example, conservative inclinations pointed in the direction of Marxist-Leninism, as the media recognize when, reporting politics in the former Soviet republics, they group Communists with other "conservatives." (Samuel Huntington, "Conservatism as an Ideology," *American Political Science Review*, Vol. 51, 1957, pp. 454-473.) In the same way, as Selden Delaney observed back in 1923, a liberal temper presumes an open mind, but one can adhere to liberal ideology with a mind that is closed or even "ultramontane." ("Radicalism or Liberalism?", *North American Review*, Vol. 217, 1923, pp. 616-627.) Delaney was thinking of Lord Acton, a devoted Catholic who was committed to liberalism; earlier, G. K. Chesterton, a converted Catholic, had expressed a similar thought: "As much as I ever did, more than I ever did, I believe in Liberalism. But there was a time of rosy innocence when I believed in Liberals." (*Orthodoxy*, Dodd Mead, 1908, p. 82.)

The ambiguous relation between doctrine and personality points to the irony of American conservatism, which many of us learned from Louis Hartz or Clinton Rossiter. (Louis Hartz, *The Liberal Tradition in America*, Harcourt Brace, 1955; Clinton Rossiter, *Conservatism in America*, Knopf, 1955.) American's oldest regime was decisively new: There was no feudal aristocracy; neither was there a Church—even the established churches in the colonies and early states were, as often as not, what Burke called the "dissidence of dissent." (*Works of Edmund Burke*, Vol. II, p. 123.) "Born equal," Americans did not have to become so. (Alexis de

Tocqueville, *Democracy in America*, Vol. II, Knopf, Vol. II, 1945, p. 101.)

Moreover, the American polity originated in a revolution, not justified in the discrete evasions of Burke's "politic, well-wrought veil," but in an appeal to natural rights. (*Works of Edmund Burke*, Vol. III, p. 255.) What the American republic came to call conservatives were—with a few exceptions like William Johnson of Connecticut—erstwhile revolutionaries who had participated in dispossessing, expelling, or repressing American Tories, and whose language, at least, often had indicated a willingness to tear up the social fabric. "I would have hanged my brother," John Adams said, "had he taken part with our enemy." American conservatives have no "ancient constitution"; the origins of our laws are only too well remembered. In the Massachusetts Constitutional Convention of 1820-1821, the aged John Adams argued for retaining a property qualification for voters, a provision, he said, instituted by "our ancestors." There must have been titters; the rule in question had been written, forty years earlier, by Adams himself. Adams the old man appealed to the ancestral wisdom of Adams the young man. (I draw both of Adams' comments, among other things, from Norman Jacobson, "The Politics of Irony," in *Principles of the Constitutional Order*, ed. Robert Utley, University Press of America, 1989, pp. 153, 158.)

So it goes. Necessarily, American conservatives are not conservative in *doctrine*; Burke, Harvey

Mansfield discovered, "does not sell well in Reagan's America." (Harvey C. Mansfield, Jr., *American's Constitutional Soul*, Johns Hopkins University Press, 1991, p. 77.) Rather, they are ideological liberals of conservative temper, whose task is not to protect the regime from alien principles, but from its own precepts, carried too far or too recklessly. At their worst, American conservatives advocate a liberalism without generosity, that liberal grace; at their best, they defend the forms and the formalities of a liberal regime against liberal neglect. (*America's Constitutional Soul*, pp. 193-208.) And that irony points to another.

Liberals—and with them the American Left—have an enormous stake in their political birthright, the antiquities and founding doctrines of the republic. (Sheldon S. Wolin, "Contract and Birthright," in *The Presence of the Past*, Johns Hopkins University Press, 1989, pp. 137-150.) In America, liberalism is a tradition and an inheritance, a bequest from the past at least as much as a triumph achieved through reason and will. Even those who have a quarrel with the Constitution characteristically invoke the Declaration of Independence, trumping the republic's second thoughts with its first principles. And while liberal theorizing is often rationalistic, in America, experience—that conservative refuge—mirrors the liberal account of the nature of politics, with governments constructed through a kind of social contract on the basis of individual rights, the separation of public and private spheres, and a more or less successful balancing of powers, interests, and claims. When I came to Rutgers' Livingston College in 1970, then a self-proclaimed bastion of radicalism and experimentation, I was fascinated to watch students, left to their own devices, create a government with a two-house legislature and a superabundance of checks and balances. Somewhat imperfectly, American custom and practice mirror liberal political philosophy; even the maddeningly abstract world of John Rawls' *A Theory of Justice*, John Schaar writes, "looks distressingly like the one we have." (*Legitimacy and the Modern State*, Transaction, 1981, p. 150.)

Not so long ago, American liberals were able to fend off an amendment excluding flag-burning from the protections of the First Amendment, relying heavily on the contention that we should not "tinker" with the Bill of Rights. That argument was doubly ironic: It passed lightly over the fact that the First Amendment itself is the result of meddling with the Constitution, and by claiming that this ancient tinkering should be exempt from present tampering, it offered one of many examples of the conservative dimension of the American liberal soul.

Almost from the beginning, Americans were a "people of paradox," adhering to both Biblical religion and modern secularism, the law of love and the ethic of self-interest, their "bittersweet" attempts at synthesis reflected in the careful ambiguities of the Declaration of Independence. (Michael Kammen, *People of Paradox*, Knopf, 1972.) And the enduring ideological anomalies of our political culture are evident in the ways in which we remember and relate to the American founding. In the ratification debate, conservatives and liberals have their favorite voices, but they also find (and often try to forget) reasons for discontent with those paladins. Political heroes, in America, come with ambiguities included.

Conservatives are ordinarily more ardent in their support for the Constitution and *The Federalist*; at least since Beard, it has been commonplace for liberal and progressive discussions of the founding to introduce at least some criticism of the drift to the right in the Federalists' design. (For example, see J. Allen Smith, *The Spirit of American Government*, Macmillan, 1912, pp. 27-39.) Unmistakably, the leading spirits among the Framers were preoccupied with order—"you must first enable the government to control the governed"—and with the protection of property. (*The Federalist*, No. 51.) They were even determined to avoid a declaration of rights and principles that might imply a criticism of convention—especially of slavery, that violation of natural right—settling instead for the relatively flat cadence of the Preamble. (Charles G. Haines, *The Making of the Constitution*, Harvard University Press, 1937, p. 392.) *The Federalist*, moreover, is an "elitist" document, at least in favoring government by the able and talented, suspecting democracy, particularly in its local and participant forms, and applauding "the total exclusion of the people in their collective capacity" from any share in government. (*The Federalist*, No. 63.)

But the Framers were also daring innovators and not overscrupulous about law. Rejecting traditional political thought in favor of the new science of politics, disregarding the Articles of Confederation, they set out to create a new, unprecedented regime, a large republic ordained in an almost absolute moment of political creativity. (Michael Lienesch, "The Constitutional Tradition: History, Political Action and Progress in American Political Thought, 1787-1793," *Journal of Politics*, No. 42, 1980, pp. 2-30.) They crafted a Constitution that is emphatically secular, not only rejecting an established church, but lacking—unlike the Declaration—any acknowledgment of divine authority. By contrast, the Framers' admiration for science and technology, shared enthusiastically by Jefferson, is reflected in the constitutional provision directing Congress to "promote the progress of science and useful arts." (Article I, Section 8.) In fact, the Framers' theorizing followed a liberal trail: They believed in natural rights and in an idea of freedom that emphasizes the individual's private capacities, treating the public good, for the most part, as an aggregate of private interests. (Joyce Appleby, *Capitalism and a New Social Order: The Republican Vision of the 1790s*, New York University Press, 1984, pp. 15-17.) Taking the struggle to master nature as a human given, they regarded acquisitiveness as a foundation of policy. Hamilton was anything but unique in arguing that narrow self-interest needs to be regulated to safeguard "orderly commerce" against "ruinous contentions." (*The Papers of Alexander Hamilton*, Vol. I, ed. Harold C. Syrett, Columbia University Press, 1961-1979, pp. 400-417.) But this sort of concern did not entail much worry about the danger of luxury. Since nature sets no limits, demand alone sets goals, and in that sense the Framers took a hesitant but crucial step in the direction of a consumer society. Moreover, despite their distaste for ancient democracy, they had no doubt that rightful authority derives from popular consent, and the Constitution establishes a politics that is at bottom democratic, albeit in the "thinned" form of voting for representatives.

Finally, the Framers rejected the ideal of a closed, coherent community in favor of an inclusive, diverse society comprising a great variety of interests—virtually as many as possible, or so Madison seemed to imply in *The Federalist*, No. 51. Their new republic was already essentially "multicultural," enfolding a plurality of sects, many divided by ancient animosities, aboriginal peoples in conflict with Europeans, and above all, the distinct and tenacious culture of slavery. (Anne Norton, *Alternative America*, University of Chicago Press, 1986.) In the Constitutional Convention, Governeur Morris sought to uphold the claims of usage and shared memory, proposing fourteen years of residence (and he might have preferred native birth) as a qualification for membership in the Senate. "Citizens of the World," Morris argued, are politically suspect; "men who can shake off their attachment to their country can never love another." As conservative doctrine, Morris's sentiments were faultless, but his proposal did not even get the vote of his state, and he was lucky to get half a loaf. No one was unkind enough to point out the irony—Morris and his fellows, after all, themselves had broken their political attachments to King and old Country—but Franklin did observe that many foreigners had supported the revolution, while many natives had opposed it. Madison, James Wilson, and Franklin all deplored the "illiberality" of Morris's motion, and it is worth noting that Madison attributes the word to all three. America, Madison contended, should want to attract "men who love liberty and are eager to partake in its blessings," and should not discourage immigrants by imposing too many disabilities. (James Madison, *Notes of Debates in the Federal Convention of 1787*, Ohio University, 1966, pp. 419-421.) In the Framers' vision, American nationality was not a given, but something subject to reshaping within the Constitution and the laws, and its watchword was not tradition, but rights and liberties.

Meanwhile, the Antifederalists, the other side of the ratification debate, have often won approval from the American liberal-left. A diverse persuasion, the Antifederalists included most of the eighteenth century's warm supporters of democracy, and their doctrine, with its emphasis on citizenship, at least resonates with contemporary ideas of political participation—especially since, like Jefferson, Antifederalists were inclined to see a need for the ongoing refounding of political community through a more or less heroic politics. Antifederalists like "Cato" and Melancton Smith warned that government under the Constitution, too complicated for ordinary citizens to understand, would be dominated by elites. Accordingly suspicious of the state and jealously protective of the prerogatives of citizens, Antifederalists were insistent advocates of a Bill of Rights. Finally, while Antifederalists respected property and were largely persuaded by the moral case for commerce, they were much more emphatic than their opponents in ranking republican self-rule above any merely economic rights or aims. All of this, in short, sounds like a program compatible with a fairly advanced sort of contemporary liberalism.

But precisely *because* of their democratic sympathies, Antifederalists were profoundly conservative, fiercely guarding the political virtue of American ways against the threat of innovation. Popular understanding, Antifederalists recognized, is local and empirical; just as ordinary citizens cannot keep close watch on a government beyond a certain scale and level of complexity, so they cannot deal with laws and policies that change too rapidly. Democratic politics, in the Antifederalist view, depends on stable laws tied to the slow pace of public deliberation. (Joshua Miller, *The Rise and Fall of Democra-*

cy in Early America, Pennsylvania State University Press, 1991, pp. 81-104.)

The Antifederalists, moreover, were not enthusiasts for purely individual liberty. They were closer to the ancient teaching that self-government consists in sharing in the life and rule of a political community. The rights they championed were less often private immunities than guarantees of a certain kind of politics—adequate representation, for example, or trial by jury, which they celebrated not so much as a protection of the rights of the accused than as the "democratic branch of the judiciary power." (Essay by a Farmer in the *Baltimore Gazette*, March 21, 1788, in Herbert Storing, ed., *The Complete Anti-Federalist*, Vol. V, University of Chicago Press, 1981, p. 38.) They regarded a coherent moral community as the basis of republicanism, as in Tocqueville's contention, based on his understanding of American Puritanism, that a moral world in which "everything is classified, systematized, foreseen and decided beforehand" provides the foundation for a political world in which "everything is agitated, disputed and uncertain." (*Democracy in America*, Vol. I, pp. 43-44.) Sharing with Federalists like Madison the hope that commerce would promote understanding and overcome privilege, they feared luxury and distrusted foreign commerce and worried, as Jefferson did, that the pursuit of private gain would overcome public spirit. (Thomas Jefferson, *Notes on the State of Virginia*, ed. William Peden, University of North Carolina Press, 1955, p.

161.) Welcoming comfort and well-being, Antifederalists defended the principle that those goods are not ends in themselves and that austerity with self-government is preferable to abundance without it.

There is an ironic side to the Antifederalists' great victory, the adoption of a Bill of Rights. Like the Virginian who wrote under the singular pseudonym "A Delegate Who Has Catched Cold," Antifederalists advocated a declaration of rights as a basis for civic education in a large republic—a sort of formal, primary schooling in politics in a regime where practice and experience no longer could be relied on to teach the essentials and dignity of citizenship. (Letter in the *Virginia Independent Chronicle*, June 25, 1788, in Storing, Vol. V, p. 273.) But the eventual Bill of Rights, shaped so much by Madison, was cast in negative, largely individualistic language, with a corresponding tendency to be read as a set of private protections against politics. In our time, one example is graphic: The Second Amendment is the most didactic provision of the Bill of Rights—and arguably of the Constitution as a whole—indicating that it proceeds from the principle that a free state depends, through a "well regulated militia," on popular service in the military. It implies, at least, a citizen's duty to serve; it surely deprecates professional soldiers. Yet in our times, the Amendment is widely read by conservatives as establishing a private right, and though contemporary liberals are critical of this interpretation, they are a long way from adopting the sterner republican teaching that the lives of citizens, like their goods, should always be at their country's command.

The American founding, in short, is an ideological muddle, full of tangled inconsistencies, especially when seen from our perspective. For most historians, John Adams is as close to an exemplar of conservatism as early America offers, just as Jefferson symbolizes liberalism, and while their theories are subtler and more ambiguous than that, the interpretation is no caricature. Yet both Jefferson and Adams served on the committee that drafted the Declaration of Independence, and both approved the Constitution, though in different ways and with different reservations. As far as our fundamental institutions are concerned, it is appropriate to paraphrase Jefferson's First Inaugural: We are all conservatives; we are all liberals.

As I have already suggested, chief among the inherited commonalities that have come to unite American liberals and conservatives is the language of individual rights, the very altar of contemporary political discourse. (Mary Ann Glendon, *Rights Talk: On the Impoverishment of Political Discourse*, Free Press, 1991.) Our political speech, in other words, is cast predominantly in the terms of liberal political philosophy, and both conservatives and liberals are more comfortable referring to political society as a device intended to meet individual needs than as a whole with claims superior to those of its parts. Tocqueville saw it: Americans, he observed, almost invariably explained their conduct in terms of "interest rightly understood," even when their actions reflected compassion and public spirit. In their speech, Tocqueville concluded, Americans were concerned to honor their "philosophy"—the doctrine that human beings are separate individuals acting from private motives—rather than their own, often nobler, qualities of soul. (*Democracy in America*, Vol. II, p. 122.) Gradually, he expected that way of talking to shape American life. And he was right.

Recently, American conservatives, while devoted to the liberal public institutions that come to them from the past, have made the defense of the "private sector" their special solicitude, hoping to wall off and preserve traditional morals, authorities, and relationships in the family, the church, and the community (just as, for a long time, many conservatives hoped to preserve the older relationship between the races). They admire, in other words, at least a version of that combination of a closed moral order with an open politics that Tocqueville saw as the *fons et origo* of things American.

The ambiguities of American politics are not escaped so easily. Inevitably, the laws intrude on the private sphere, regulating property, defining enforceable rights and obligations, and marking off the limits of private authority. Since the ruling precept of the laws is what Tocqueville called the "spirit of liberty," even conservatives upholding moral obligations are apt to speak in terms of personal rights. Opponents of abortion, for example, appeal to a "right to life," not a duty to nurture, and recent advertising on that side of the question refers to life as a "beautiful choice," virtually conceding a good deal of that right to choose that has been their opponents' stock in trade.

The ironies of American conservatism, however, are most evident in economic life. In the United States, capitalism and the market are pillars of established authority, and in that sense it is no surprise that for most of our history, the championship of economic liberty—relatively unregulated competition for wealth—has been a centerpiece of conservative doctrine. But the market is anything but conservative: It teaches that property is acquired not for transmission to succeeding generations, but for gain in exchange. In market capitalism, the view of property is dynamic, bound up with growth and continuous transformation, (Leo Strauss, *Natural Right and History*, University of Chicago Press, 1953, p. 245.) The logic of the market reduces qualities to quantities, and especially to the standard of money. At the "bottom line," capitalism is utterly disdainful of tradition or of any relationships that cannot pass the test of profitability. Recently, speaking of the chronic need to refound corporations, Albert J. Dunlap, Chief Executive Officer of the Scott Paper Company, remarked that "You must get rid of the people who represent the old culture . . . and you have to get rid of all the old symbols." (*New York Times*, August 15, 1944, p. D1.) The moral language of the market does not speak of virtues but of values, a set of preferences molded by desire and opinion. "The Value or Worth of a man," Hobbes proclaimed, "is as of all things, his Price, that is to say, so much as would be given for the use of his Power; and therefore is not a thing absolute; but a thing dependent upon the need and judgment of another." (*Leviathan*, Part I, ch. 10.) In a word, the catechism of the market is relativism, its foundations resting on the sands of supply and demand.

This doctrine cannot be confined to economics, more or less narrowly defined; encouraging individualism, capitalism presumes and legitimates the "sovereignty of the passions." (Joseph Cropsey, *Political Philosophy and the Issues of Politics*, University of Chicago Press, 1977, p. 29.) The market values and rewards mobility, human beings who anticipate and respond freely to the currents of change. Its preferred social unit is the relatively free-floating individual or one-worker household, and it regards attachments to community, to extended family, or to craft as "frictional," if not essentially irrational. Historically, capitalism saw marriage and family as useful stimuli to ambition that also gave employees' lives a desirable stability. Increasingly, however, corporate America is inclined to view marriage as a problem involving possible impediments to mobility. At best, hiring policy is no longer a reliable ally of the family, and it is probably more accurate to say, as Elizabeth Fox-Genovese does, that economic forces and technology are "tolerating, when not financing, the destruction of the family, church and every other institution that aspires to a measure of autonomy." ("From Separate Spheres to Dangerous Streets: Postmodern Feminism and the Problem of Order," *Social Research*, Vol. 60, 1993, pp. 235-254.) In other words, the conservative effort to defend both traditional values and unregulated capitalism amounts to trying to square a moral circle. (Christopher Lasch, "Traditional Values: Left, Right and Wrong," *Harpers*, September, 1986, p. 14.)

For a long time, modern American conservatism was held together by anticommunism and by the need to combat an ascendant liberalism, both of which militated against overniceness in relation to allies, present or potential. (E. J. Dionne, Jr., *Why Americans Hate Politics*, Simon and Schuster, 1991, pp. 157-169.) Today, by contrast, greater strength on the right and the collapse of the Soviet empire make conservatives readier to air their disagreements in public. In intellectual circles, of course, differences between conservatives have long been evident and fundamental. On the libertarian side, Robert Nozick promotes a radically individualistic doctrine of rights, rooted in the philosophy of liberals like Locke, carried to an extreme in its suspicion of authority. (*Anarchy, State and Utopia*, Basic Books, 1974.) By contrast, from a position closer to historic conservatism, Harvey Mansfield rejoins that libertarian zeal for the "sovereignty of the self" threatens the "self-government of the self," an ideal that requires moral character, pride, and the willingness to sacrifice one's personal interests and liberties for one's country, the political whole of which personal freedoms are a part. (*America's Constitutional Soul*, pp. 77, 82-83.) And in political practice, there are now regular, frequently bitter contests that pit social conservatives of various sorts—religious rightists are only the most visible—against their more economistic and libertarian rivals, or against each other. The discord is escalating beyond ambiguity; the new thunder on the right may prove to be rumblings along the fault lines of American conservatism.

But of course, liberals have parallel problems of their own. Modern liberals have always been ambivalent about market capitalism. They value the dynamic commercial economy which, after all, was largely a liberal invention, looking to it to provide abundance, appreciating its contribution to the easing of human life, and hoping for the well-being that prompts generosity. And like earlier liberals, they admire it for breaking down narrowness, exclusiveness, and prejudice, opening communities to new ideas and influences, and linking peoples in the bonds of trade and acquaintance. On the other hand, where the founders of liberalism allowed themselves to hope that free competition would limit the range and permanence of inequalities, by the mid-nineteenth century their successors learned that the market permits the development of towering inequalities, with differences of power deriving from large-scale institutions at least as alarming as disparities of wealth. Private power modifies, if it does not escape, the logic of competition which—in economics and in its influence on government—has long since become oligopolistic, the power of the few constraining the opportunities of the many. Moreover, modern liberalism also recognizes that the combination of inequality with instability—especially the threat of unemployment—increases social insecurity and the fear of indignity. That in turn accentuates the dark side of market psychology: It prods human beings toward becoming more unambiguously self-interested and grasping, and hence exclusive and lacking in sympathy, concerned only for their own, narrowly defined. In other words, free market liberalism endangers liberality; historic liberal doctrine threatens the liberal soul. (Reinhold Niebuhr, "Liberalism, Illusions and Realities," *New Republic*, July 4, 1955, pp. 11-13.)

This tension increasingly has been accentuated by the weakening of the moral and social foundations of liberal politics. The American Constitution, of course, gives no formal support to any social institution other than property: Like the founders of liberalism generally, the American Framers were inclined to think that, whenever possible, government should leave social life and moral education to the devices of others. Any government efforts to shape the soul entail threats to liberty; the great liberal teachers were more concerned to keep religion and concern for the soul from dominating political life, preferring religions and souls that are law-abiding and willing to surrender their this-worldly claims to rule. On liberal principles, moreover, public life is a sphere in which nominal equals are governed on the basis of reason and consent; the private sphere includes authorities established without consent and rules often tailored to human emotion. Intervention in private life, consequently, requires a liberal public authority to violate either its own principles or those of the private order, so that it is far less troublesome to leave the two spheres separate.

Both the Framers and their opponents took it for granted, however, that families, churches, local communities, and schools would nurture and develop the civil sentiments and decencies. A liberal polity rests on rather definite moral premises. In the first place, it relies on civility and tolerance, and hence trust and reasonable personal security, manifested through citizens who keep their promises and fulfill their obligations even when doing so no longer seems in their interest. The laws can help protect that last excellence—the Constitution demands that states respect the "obligation of contracts" (Article 1, section 10)—but the risk of being caught and punished affords only an inadequate guarantee; all human beings are tempted by the calculation that the potential gains from breaking a rule outweigh the chances of being detected. *Strong* security for pledges demands the support of personal convictions, and perhaps of higher authority. ("Promises, covenants and oaths, which are the bonds of human society," Locke wrote, "can have no hold upon an atheist." *Letter Concerning Toleration*, ed. Patrick Romanell, Bobbs Merrill, 1955, p. 52.) Second, a truly liberal citizen is generous-spirited, and even those liberal theorists who regarded benevolence as part of a "moral sense" or "instinct" recognized that it is a quality that requires cultivation through appropriate doctrines and ways of life. Any damage to the private order, consequently, endangers the basis of liberal citizenship. (William Galston, "Public Morality and Religion in the Liberal State," *PS*, Vol. 19, 1986, pp. 822-824.) By the late nineteenth century, liberal voices were warning that those institutions were becoming embattled and too often overthrown by the dynamics of modern life.

Willy-nilly, more and more liberals felt compelled toward the task of economic and social reconstruction, invoking government to safeguard and amplify a lifeworld suited to the liberal spirit. (John Dewey, *Individualism Old and New*, Minton and Balch, 1930.) This adventure drew on archetypically liberal qualities—sympathy and inclusiveness, for example, as well as a disposition to innovate—but it also moved into areas and policies traditionally associated with conservatism. Herbert Croly appealed to Hamilton with more enthusiasm than he showed for Jefferson, and the leaders we now regard as the founders of modern liberalism typically preferred to call themselves "Progressives" to avoid association with radical individualism and the nightwatchman state. (Herbert Croly, *The Promise of American Life*, Macmillan, 1911, pp. 29, 37-46.) In many ways, the beginning of the Progressive era was signalled by Frederick Jackson Turner's warning of the passing of an American tradition, the end of the frontier that had provided, Turner argued, the environmental basis of American democracy. Nothing epitomizes Progressive concerns more than the policy of conservation, and in general, Progressives hoped to refurbish the rough equality, full employment, and moral coherence they remembered in the American past. And they were surely moralists, albeit of a bourgeois sort. Theodore Roosevelt, Mencken observed, had the instincts of a "property-owning Tory" even when he adopted liberal postures; "no one ever heard him make an argument for the rights of the citizen; his eloquence was always expended in expounding the duties of the citizen." (H. L. Mencken, *Prejudices: Second Series*, Knopf, 1920, pp. 121-123.)

It should be emphasized, however, that Progressives were attempting to conserve the moral basis of a liberal society. They distrusted traditional, merely customary, or ethnic institutions and cultures, and even those who were most welcoming toward "hyphenated" Americans wanted to liberate individuals from the prejudices of locality or the past. They called the forms and proprieties into question, seeking to reform and refound social institutions on liberal bases—choice, reason, or science—using schools as a key to overcoming "cultural lag" and working to produce "habits of mind and character . . . that are somewhere near even with the actual movement of events." (John Dewey, *Liberalism and Social Action*, Putnam, 1935, pp. 58-62, 75-76.)

As that indicates, modern liberals began with confidence in the moral direction of history, convinced that change and science work to promote cooperation and democracy. They saw little difficulty, consequently, in reconciling their moralism with the relativism that was their characteristic weapon against established institutions, (Eric Goldman, *Rendezvous with Destiny*, Knopf, 1952.) The relativity of cultures and codes was thought virtually to entail a broad tolerance or even egalitarianism—a notion similar to the conceit that, paradoxically buttressed by the authority of Nietzsche, one finds so often in universities today. (Allan Bloom, *The Closing of the American Mind*, Simon and Schuster, 1987, pp. 25, 202-204, 225-226, 228-229.) But the Progressive period and our own times are separated by the era of totalitarianism and total war.

Experience has made contemporary liberals much more skeptical about technology and the redemptive logic of history; these days, historicism speaks about history's ineluctabilities, not its promise. Among political philosophers, John Dewey enjoys a new vogue, but his admirers lack the serene assurance of Dewey's faith in science when they are not, like Richard Rorty, agnostics or unbelievers. (Charles Anderson, "Pragmatism and Liberalism, Rationalism and Irrationalism: A Response to Richard Rorty," *Polity*, Vol. 23, 1991, pp. 360-363.) There is no shortage of reasons for this incertitude.

Economic inequalities of wealth and power have grown even more staggering, enough to raise serious questions about the possibilities of liberal citizenship. Observation taught Jefferson that economic inequality is tolerably compatible with political equality when work at a "comfortable subsistence" is sufficiently certain that no worker feels dependent on a particular employer. (Letter to John Adams, Oct. 28, 1813, *Life and Selected Writings*, p. 633.) Today, by contrast, socially adequate jobs are scarce, and with corporations celebrating "downsizing," are insecure even for those who have them. Americans are feeling pressed, growing less generous and more anxious to defend their own. The very affluent increasingly feel able and driven to insulate themselves from the problems of other Americans; society seems to be dividing into the exempt and the trapped. (Robert Reich, "The Secession of the Successful," *New York Times Magazine*, Jan. 20, 1991, p. 17ff.) Meanwhile, more and more liberals worry about crime, the apparent rise of domestic violence and abuse, and the increase in social isolation and self-concern.

All of this reinforces the tendency of liberals—joined by conservatives more often than the right likes to admit—to look to government to redress the order of things. In economics, at least, liberals have something like a standard for policy—full employment at adequate wages—however difficult it is to achieve in practice (and however many differences there are between liberals—often bitter ones—about the best road to that goal). Socially, however, contemporary liberals are far less willing than their predecessors to establish a public definition of a desirable family or social order. In part, this reflects a greater awareness of marginal groups and cultures, combined with a generous liberal desire to include them in the body politic; there is simply a lot more *pluribus*, these days, in the American *unum*. And since liberals tend to be defenders of the freedom of "lifestyle," a great many are unwilling to "stigmatize" single-parent families or other unorthodox unions. (As the number of such families grows, moreover, political leaders also have reason to hesitate about giving offense, as Dan Quayle learned.) As a result, liberals, warmly willing to help single-parent families, are apt to be left with only a narrowly economic basis for doing so; conservatives, with every reason to recognize the difficulties under which single parents operate, are just as likely to be unwilling to do more than blame them.

It makes matters worse that liberals have become less enthusiastic about democratic politics, and not only because of their experience in recent elections. Since marginal and vulnerable groups have a more or less desperate stake in supportive public policy, liberals have been unwilling to leave them to the vagaries of majority opinion, especially in these crabbed times. Instead, liberals have developed the habit of setting themselves to establish such policies as rights, relatively immune to politics (a process that almost all of us participate in where our own interests are concerned).

This parallels the ironic fact that the more individuals are dwarfed by private power on one hand and the state on the other, and the clearer it becomes that a free spirit depends on attachments and social supports, the more liberals—to say nothing of right-wing libertarians or Americans generally—seem to insist on their belief in the moral autonomy of the individual. Robert Bellah and his associates found, in fact, that Americans have virtually no moral language other than individualism. (Robert N. Bellah, Richard Madsen, William M. Sullivan, Ann Swidler, and Steven Tipton, *Habits of the Heart: Individualism and Commitment in American Life*, University of California Press, 1982.) The putative freedom of an inner world, in other words, is invoked as a defense and consolation against an increasingly constraining outer one. (George Kateb, *The Inner Ocean*, Cornell University Press, 1992.)

It is part of this process that, unlike the founders of liberalism, contemporary theorists do not attempt to root the "priority" of individual liberty in nature. (John Rawls, *A Theory of Justice*, pp. 509, 541-548.) Quite the contrary, the current tendency is to diminish or reject the idea of human nature because it constitutes a restraint on liberty. The human self, in this persuasion, cannot be ruled rightly by any norm external to itself; human beings are bound only by principles of their own making. (Marvin Zetterbaum, "Self and Subjectivity in Political Theory," *Review of Politics*, Vol. 44, 1982, pp. 59-82.) Postmodernism and deconstructionism are only a new stage in the logic of this argument, appealing to liberals because, irreverent toward canonical authority, they seem to affirm a more inclusive liberty.

Even on its own terms, however, this line of argument moralizes and contributes to social fragmentation, and individuals left alone are no match for the dominations and powers of the time. In fact, the most strident voices on today's American liberal-left recognize that, like the market in material goods, the free marketplace of ideas does not guarantee social justice and can work to the detriment of culturally disadvantaged groups. Often ham-handed and self-interested, the demand for "political correctness" includes a largely appropriate insistence on civility and respect toward women and toward minority races and sexual orientations. Yet ironically, this consideration is not ordinarily extended to others; those who require civil speech in the first set of cases resist any limit on "authentic" self-expression everywhere else.

As this hints, avant-garde liberalism has at best an uneasy relationship to democracy. Postmodern and deconstructionist teachings, for example, are disdainful of common modes of speech and understanding. While far from conservative in principle, in practice thinkers who follow Derrida disparage the possibilities of political change in a way that recalls Burke. (William Corlett, *Community Without Unity*, Duke University Press, 1989, pp. 118-141.) Most important, their emphasis on the difference between human subjects and cultures, an old conservative set piece, is at poles with the principle of equality, the cornerstone of democratic life. (Sheldon S. Wolin, "Democracy, Difference and Recognition," *Political Theory*, Vol. 21, 1993, pp. 466, 481.)

Like their conservative rivals, American liberals are being torn by their own culture war, one that ranges economic egalitarians, often relatively conservative in social terms, against the libertarian-to-nihilist strain of the cultural left. (Bernard Avishai, "The Pursuit of Happiness and Other 'Preferences,'" *Dissent*, Vol. 31, 1984, pp. 482-484.). All too visible in the Clinton administration, that conflict is another illustration of how problematical historic ideologies are as guides to American politics.

Liberal and conservative temperaments will always be with us, but liberal and conservative doctrines have become scrambled when they are not simply played out, although there are formidable obstacles to formulating a more adequate set of alternatives. If I have spent more time discussing the liberals' dilemma, it is partly because my heritage runs in their direction, but also because I am persuaded that even cultural conservatives are too willing to accommodate to the market's relativistic dynamics. (Leslie Kaufman, "Life Beyond God,"

New York Times Magazine, Oct. 16, 1994, p. 46ff.) Economic life has a kind of primacy: As Thoreau warned us, our ways of *getting* a living will always have a shaping effect on our ways of living. ("Life Without Principle," in *Works of Henry David Thoreau*, ed. Henry Seidel Canby, Houghton Mifflin, 1946, p. 813.) But beyond economics, any effort to revitalize American politics also will have to deal broadly with civil society, the private foundations of public life. And Michael Sandel is right: We are becoming "more entangled, but less attached," personally "unencumbered" but caught in a network of interdependencies. (Michael Sandel, "The Procedural Republic and the Unencumbered Self" in Tracy Strong, ed., *The Self and the Political Order*, New York University Press, 1992, p. 92.) Seriously addressed, restoring or reconstructing the private order is bound to run up against deeply entrenched parts of the way we live—the pace of change, the scale of economic and cultural life, personal mobility, even the dream of affluence.

Understandably, most of our political leaders prefer to talk at the problem, not the worst idea, since in a republic persuasion needs to precede law. But even when conservative and liberal speakers abandon the language of rights, they invoke "values," the idiom of the market, asking us for better preferences rather than improved but demanding ways of living. Our older Biblical language—the first grammar of American life—speaks of virtues and of righteousness, qualities beyond choosing, bound up with the fundamental order of things. From that teaching, we learned to regard our rights as unalienable, not made by us nor subject to our surrendering. But we also were taught that community is a fact of life: Human beings are parts of nature, stewards and not masters, and subject to a law that assigns them duties to nature and to each other. For both liberals and conservatives, reclaiming that voice is a first step toward rearticulating the inner dialogue—the ambiguity and irony—that is the soul of a liberal republic.